Reaching for God

Reaching for God
The Benedictine Oblate Way of Life

Roberta Werner, OSB

LITURGICAL PRESS
Collegeville, Minnesota

www.litpress.org

Cover design by Jodi Hendrickson. Cover image: ThinkStock.

Excerpts from documents of the Second Vatican Council are from *The Documents of Vatican II*, edited by Walter M. Abbott ©1966 (America Press). Used by permission.

Excerpts from the Rule are taken from *Rule of Saint Benedict 1980*, edited by Timothy Fry © 1981 (Liturgical Press).

Excerpts from *A Handbook for Directors of Benedictine Oblates* (Saint Meinrad, IN: Abbey Press, 2000) are used with permission of the NAABOD.

Scripture texts in this work are taken from the *New Revised Standard Version Bible* © 1989, Division of Christian Education of the National Council of the Churches of Christ in the United States of America. Used by permission. All rights reserved.

1   2   3   4   5   6   7   8   9

Library of Congress Cataloging-in-Publication Data

Werner, Roberta.
    Reaching for God : the Benedictine Oblate way of life / Roberta Werner, OSB.
      pages cm
    Includes bibliographical references.
    ISBN 978-0-8146-3551-3 — ISBN 978-0-8146-3576-6 (e-book)
    1. Benedictines—Spiritual life.   I. Title.
  BX3003.W47   2013
  255'.1—dc23   2012048197

Dedication

I dedicate this book to Pope John XXIII who listened to the Holy Spirit and whose positive, hope-filled attitude, along with his concern for the spiritual needs of the present time, gave us Vatican II with its unique and valued documents referring to the importance of the laity as members of the church and as a key and irreplaceable element in the work of the church and the world.

In memory of my parents and grandparents whose love and self-giving were models of true Gospel-living and Christian witness to the God who is unconditional Love.

For all who cannot ease their longing and for all who seek and reach for our mysterious God Who promised to be with us always.

Contents

Acknowledgments

My deepest gratitude to my Benedictine Community of Saint Benedict's Monastery in St. Joseph, Minnesota, for initially inviting me to write this book, and providing me with the time, physical space, and materials to do so. My heartfelt thanks go out to every Benedictine oblate in the world, but especially to the oblates of my Benedictine monastery who are a constant inspiration to me in the way they truly live the Rule of Benedict in the secular world. A special thanks to my oblate discussion group, which is an unending source of spiritual enrichment and joy. My gratitude extends to all authors on Benedictine spirituality who have mined the treasures of Benedict's Rule and shared them with the world. I am also grateful to Peter Dwyer and Hans Christoffersen of the Liturgical Press for their continued interest in this manuscript throughout its metamorphosis, and to Lauren L. Murphy and Nicole Werner, my editors at Liturgical Press.

In conclusion I give my love and thanks to all of my Benedictine sisters, my family, and friends whose presence in my life manifests God in so many ways.

May each of us keep our ears and hearts open to our all-loving God whose Spirit continues to renew the earth and all who live on our planet.

Introduction

Teilhard de Chardin once wrote: "We are not human beings having a spiritual experience. We are spiritual beings having a human experience." When we are unaware of that profound truth and start to live shallow lives bogged down in materialistic pursuits, the sense that "there must be something more" is with us daily. So many people look for quick fixes to their unhappiness. In their search for meaning, they turn to drugs, alcohol, sex, constant activity, new self-help programs, unending work, mindless, constant entertainment, and the like. They have never learned what Karl Rahner put so well: "In the torment of the insufficiency of everything attainable we eventually learn that here, in this life, all symphonies remain unfinished." Having come face-to-face with that realization—having acknowledged that, plus our longing for meaning—we have then reached the point where we can discover (or rediscover) who we really are, where we are really going, and whether or not we want to change our path. It is at that point in life that we are ready to exchange shallowness and superficial living for depth and meaning and endeavors that are worthy of us.

Have you reached that stage in life? If you are restless, feeling "out-of-joint" and unfulfilled; if you are reaching for that unknown Something or Someone that can help to anchor you at the same time as it challenges you, enriches you, and plunges you into Mystery, you may find the answer here, in this book—in this spirituality. Whether or not you are aware of it, the "Someone" you are seeking is God, and Saint Benedict found a path to a fruitful, rich life in God that has proved itself over the centuries—that is, from the sixth century into our twenty-first. In his Prologue to the Rule, Benedict asks, "Is there anyone here who yearns for life and desires to see good days? (Ps 34[34]:13)" (RB Prol. 15). He then invites us to open our eyes and ears to God's invitation through Scripture and through Benedict's own loving guidance in the Rule, which he wrote for the good of all, out of love. Do not be confused or daunted by the term "rule." It is not some harsh, unyielding dictum but an invitation to follow a prescribed path, to use a type of framework, a trellis structure through which you can grow to personal fulfillment and a meaningful life.

If you are searching for a *why* and a purpose in your life—if you are aching for a sense of fulfillment, a feeling of belonging, a need for wholeness—this book may help you find the way. In their personal search for meaning, many men and women have found the answer by living a life based on Benedictine spirituality. They found their spiritual home in their affiliation with Benedictine monasteries as oblates. In the Benedictine family of their choice, and through their monastic connection, they sought and continue to seek God together in the company of thousands of others. This book will tell you both the why and the how of that path to meaning.

The reawakening and resurgence of Benedictine spirituality for the laity has produced many recent books on this subject. Some of them address the Rule of Benedict directly in the form of new translations, others combine the quotation of the Rule with commentaries, and some publications address oblates of Saint Benedict directly. There are books with essays by oblates and books about prominent oblates. This book is a compendium, a type of integration-convergence, of Benedictine spirituality for the layperson. In its comprehensiveness, this book brings together, in one volume, the essence of Benedictine spirituality: its history, its relevance through the ages into the present century, and its ongoing values for living a meaningful life. It gives the history of lay connections to Benedictine monasteries from their inception as it addresses Benedictine spirituality in the form of lay oblation. This book confirms the importance of the laity in the work of the church and the world as stated in the documents of Vatican II, offering the reader an opportunity to connect with the documents' important affirmations of the laity's role in spreading the Good News about salvation.

At the same time as it invites the layperson into the rich spiritual life of a Benedictine oblate, this book provides many bibliographical resources for the reader's spiritual life in general. Accessing these, in addition to the websites and additional materials included, offers a good foundation for the reader's continuing personal spiritual growth. There are also examples of prayer and *lectio,* which are applicable to any spiritual life and can enrich the mind and heart.

Benedict's wisdom, offered through his Rule, has proved itself by enduring through every age since its birth. When we live in a "throw-away" culture such as ours; when the new "toy" we bought is suggested to be obsolete just weeks after our purchase; when the new fad for healing and the new self-help books disappoint; when we look for something that has proved itself to be stable enough to depend on for the long haul, we can trust Benedictine spirituality. Saint Benedict knew human nature. He lived in a time of great upheaval, unrest, spiritual dissolution. He found the answer to a meaningful life through Scripture, prayer, and specific life values and practices. His answer just might be yours as well. Take a peek into this book and be surprised and delighted to find a piece of yourself in Benedict's wise recognition of and approach to humanity. As Benedict would say, "That in all things God may be glorified."

CHAPTER 1

Benedictine Spirituality as Related to Oblate Life/Living

The Essence of Benedictine Spirituality

The Benedictine goal is to seek God. Benedictine life is fueled by Scripture and prayer and an effort to see and find God in each person and experience in daily life. Every person is to be treated as Christ and all material things are to be treated with respect and care. Life is to be lived in moderation with a healthy balance between work and prayer. Benedictines are to listen in loving obedience to the will of God as they have perceived it in their prayer, *lectio*, and life events. They live the Rule and the Christian life in community with other God-committed individuals and continue their efforts at conversion of heart. Fidelity in faith and stability of heart and place are also key aspects of Benedictine life. Benedictine spirituality advises and points the way to living the Christian life to its fullest extent by deepening the person's relationship to God and developing a personal relationship/friendship with Jesus Christ. The Benedictine tries to live in the present in prayerful and loving connection to God and family, as well as to his or her religious and civic community.

What/Who Is an Oblate?

Oblates are Christian women and men who affiliate with a Benedictine monastic community and consider the monastery their spiritual home. Oblates study the Rule of Benedict as a spiritual guide and live its spirit in their daily lives in whichever way their unique situations permit them to adapt it. They do what they can to be witnesses to Christ by word and example. They make a commitment

1

to follow and be shaped by Benedictine spirituality. Oblates try to live the ordinary in an extraordinary way, fueled by the Gospel of Christ in the midst of a secular and often Godless society. Oblates can be a leaven for good in the midst of their family and civic and church communities, and they become an extension of their monastic family for a world that does not know God and is often lost in darkness.

Why Become an Oblate?

Our culture is steeped in materialism and is often antispiritual. Oblates have found that living the shallow life is unsatisfactory. Instead, they seek God and a deeper relationship with Christ by choosing to connect themselves to a spiritual home—a Benedictine community committed to living out the Gospel values according to the Rule of Benedict. Christians who choose to become oblates are attracted to Benedictine values of living a life centered in God, the present moment, wholeness, moderation, prayer, and the Gospel. Oblates can establish a network of relationships and friendships with the monks, brothers, and sisters at their monastic communities and with other oblates who support and enrich their life experiences. They have an opportunity for continuous deepening of their spirituality through oblate meetings, renewal days, and participation in spirituality center programs and other offerings at their chosen monastery. Oblates are also included in the daily prayers of the monastic community. In this time of severed family bonds, declining family life, and eroded community life, oblates know that their monastic home is stable and will always be there for them despite an ever-changing world. Oblates grow in their awareness of God's unconditional love as they start to live the Rule of Benedict. They become more deeply aware of the truth of a personal God who is involved in all creation and is by nature operative in their daily lives. They begin to experience the undeniable fact that they, and all who exist, are God's beloved. They enrich their spiritual lives through their connection with God's presence in the Benedictine community of their choice.

The Partnership of Oblate and Monastery

In choosing to become an oblate, Christians select a community to help them to live out the promise of their baptism in a more serious way. We are all on a spiritual journey, which, because of our weaknesses, includes constant conversion and is basically a process of continuous renewal. The Benedictine community that the oblate chooses as a spiritual home is a source of prayerful support and offers spiritual resources through activities, special events, and both digital and print publications. The monastery welcomes oblates to participate in its daily Eucharist, Divine Office, and special occasions. It shares its Benedictine way of life through mailings, e-mails, Facebook, and other methods of contact and also includes the needs of oblates and community in its general communications and prayer.

Oblates are an extension of the monastery to a needy world. Their commitment to living Benedictine spirituality makes them a presence for good wherever they are. They love their monastery and are advocates for its values and spiritual culture/life. They support the monastic community in prayer and are one of its links to the world of work, family, church, and civic communities to which the oblates try to bring peace, justice, love, and all the elements of their learned Benedictine values.

CHAPTER 2

The Rule of Benedict
The Source of Benedictine Spirituality

History of Saint Benedict and the Rule

Saint Benedict was born in Nursia, Italy, ca. AD 480. As a young man he was sent to Rome to study the liberal arts. He became disenchanted with the decadence around him so he left Rome and eventually took residence in a narrow cave in a mountainous area called Subiaco. There he lived in solitude for three years, choosing to rely on God in great trust. When Benedict was discovered by the local people he was soon recognized for his holiness. He began to instruct them about the spiritual life and they, in turn, shared food with him.

Disciples continued to seek Benedict for his spiritual wisdom and eventually a group of local monks asked him to be their abbot. He was reluctant to accept the invitation because they were an undisciplined group and he doubted that they really sought to reform. When they persisted he accepted their invitation. Eventually the monks became more and more resistant to Benedict's efforts at reform and tried to kill him with poison.

He was miraculously spared. Benedict left those monks and returned to his hermit life. His holiness, manifested "in signs and wonders,"[1] became widely known and soon many men joined him to devote themselves to God. Ultimately he established twelve monasteries in the area around Subiaco, each housing an abbot and twelve monks. The envy and vicious deeds of a jealous local priest led Benedict to leave Subiaco with a small group of monks. They settled at Monte Cassino, seventy miles south of Rome, where he eventually wrote the Rule. Benedict died in AD 547.

The Rule of Benedict has its foundation in the Bible and is the result of Saint Benedict's long life of prayer, meditation, lived experience, and knowledge of other monastic traditions. In his Rule, Benedict shares his profound insights into life as he deals with the daily. The Rule is a guide for all who really search for God and it reflects Benedict's love of God and knowledge of human nature as it deals with the balancing of work and prayer, relationships, mindfulness of the uniqueness and need of each individual, reverence and respect for material things (stewardship), authority/leadership and community, hospitality, silence, worship and study, and aspects of spiritual and psychological growth. It provides a structure, a guide for living that is rooted in Christ and mindful of our ordinary lives and their connections to the variety of communities of which we are a part—e.g., family, church, workplace, civic and religious organizations, neighborhoods, and towns/cities.

The Rule and Oblate Living

Saint Benedict's Rule is "a school for the Lord's service" (RB Prol. 45).[2] It urges us and tells us how to live a life centered in Christ. It offers the oblate "nothing harsh, nothing burdensome" (RB Prol. 46) and is written by a man who has found God, loves us and God, and shows us how to listen for and find God in our daily lives.

An oblate who has decided to live according to the Rule of Benedict is basically embracing the Christian life in all its fullness. She or he will try to "prefer nothing to Christ" and will try to live that mandate every day, wherever or with whomever she or he is. The oblate will be fueled by prayer and Scripture and will find that the Rule is an aid to remembering the meaning of life and ordering personal priorities in living life.

Renowned Witnesses to Oblate Living

Throughout the centuries, the Rule of Benedict has inspired not only monastics but also lay Christians to live a life of wholeness and holiness. Saint Thomas More was an oblate who had the courage to defy Henry VIII rather than to deny truth. Closer to our own time, Dorothy Day (1897–1980), founder of the Catholic Worker, Jacques Maritain, French philosopher, and Paul Claudel, French poet and playwright, found their roles as oblates to bear fruit in their daily lives.

Dorothy Day was drawn to the Benedictine values of balance between work, prayer, hospitality, community, and seeing Christ in all people. One of Day's coworkers is quoted as saying: "I am sure that without the influence of the Benedictines that there would be very little in the Catholic Worker Movement—For from the Benedictines we got the ideal of Hospitality—Guest Houses—Forming Communes—Liturgical Prayer. Take these away and there is very little in the Catholic Worker Program."[3] Oblate Rita McClain Tybor notes that she was moved by Dorothy Day's commitment to prayer. She quotes Eileen Egan who wrote of Day: "Her fidelity to prayer was her path to the transformation called for by the witness of peace, voluntary poverty, and mercy to the needy."[4] Dorothy Day began each day with prayer. Early in the morning she could be found faithfully praying the psalms. She said when she was in her seventies: "More and more I see [that] prayer is the answer. It is the clasp of the hand, the joy and keen delight in the consciousness of that Other. Indeed it is like falling in love."[5] As an oblate, Dorothy Day lived the Rule to the point of sanctity.

Jacques Maritain, a renowned philosopher, writer, and teacher, and his wife Raïssa, an internationally known philosopher, poet, and mystic, were both Benedictine oblates. Their household had "a quasi-monastic horarium including daily Mass, the Liturgy of the Hours, times for work, meals, music, conversation, and reading."[6] The Maritains "opened their lives and homes to the needs of others. They loved the Church. In an important sense, they were Benedictine children, obedient and faithful listeners, whose lives stayed fully open to transformation until their very last days."[7] Their lifelong search for truth and God, and their quest for deep philosophical as well as theological answers to questions of faith, are of worldwide note. In early 2011 a Vatican news agency reported that the Maritain's beatification process would begin.[8]

Paul Claudel: Some Specifics about One Oblate's Spiritual Journey

Paul Claudel was a poet, playwright, diplomat, mystic, and an oblate of Saint Benedict. The specifics of his life and spiritual journey are included here to give a more detailed idea of the path someone took to reach and embrace the Benedictine oblate way of life.

Paul Claudel was born at Villeneuve, France, on the border between the provinces of Champagne and the Ile-de-France on August 6, 1868. He died in Paris on February 23, 1955. His father was a civil servant so Paul received his early education in various schools, depending on the area to which his father was assigned. When the family moved to Paris in 1882, Paul was enrolled in the Lycée Louis-le-Grand where he won a first prize in oratory. Paul's family was Catholic by tradition but the Claudels were basically indifferent toward the church. Paul received only the basic religious instruction needed to prepare him for his First Communion.

Claudel's education in Paris was grounded in the philosophies of materialism, determinism, and positivism, all of which contend that sense perceptions are the only admissible basis of human knowledge and precise thought. These doctrines did not satisfy Claudel as an answer to his constant need to understand the *why* of life. He was always an avid reader, devouring Shakespeare, Dante, and Virgil (and later Aristotle, Saint Thomas Aquinas, and John Henry Newman), along with many other great authors. He credits Rimbaud with revealing the supernatural to him as a reality. After reading Arthur Rimbaud, the eighteen-year-old Claudel attended Christmas services at Notre Dame Cathedral in Paris (1886). There he had a mystical experience that confirmed for him that there was a living God who was personal. He could now say, "I believe."

For four more years after this experience, Claudel struggled with intellectual objections which impeded his spiritual progress. He had been taught to be skeptical and to doubt, to know that everything in the world could be explained by the laws of science. Now he began to study the Bible, the history of the church, and liturgy. Of the struggle, he wrote: "And I was before You like a wrestler who bends, / Not that he thinks himself weak but because the other is stronger."[9] During these four years he also studied law and political science, wrote plays and poetry, and entered the French diplomatic service.

By Christmas 1890, his "conversion" to Catholicism was complete and at Notre Dame Cathedral he received the Eucharist for the second time in his life. From 1893 to 1899, Claudel held junior consular posts in New York, Boston, and Shanghai. In 1899 he returned to France by way of Syria and Palestine.

Claudel had a diplomatic leave in the year 1900. His longing for God was intense and he was thinking of leaving diplomacy and entering religious life. He made a retreat at the Benedictine Abbey of Solesmes, then went to the Benedictine Abbey of Ligugé where he spent eight days in retreat. There the Benedictines dissuaded him from entering religious life and helped him realize that he would serve the church better by remaining "in the world." In a sense Claudel now felt rejected by God and experienced spiritual turmoil. He had led a life of sacrifice and self-denial; he had even decided to give up his gift of art. Why would God not want him? Yet, since he always remained a man of God, he became a Benedictine oblate. A friend wrote of Claudel: "Nothing mattered to this man of strong will and faith except his longing to partake in the power of eternal love."

Claudel's diplomatic career continued as did his literary output. He went back to China, returned to Europe in 1905, married Reine Sainte-Marie-Perrin in 1906, then returned with her to China. In 1908 he was named consul in Prague; 1911, consul at Frankfurt. He was sent to Hamburg in 1913 only to be recalled at the outbreak of the war. From 1914 to 1916, Claudel was in Bordeaux, while also lecturing in Switzerland and Italy. In 1917 he was chargé d'affaires for Rio de Janeiro and traveled in Brazil. In 1919 he left for Denmark. Between the years of 1921 and 1927 he was the French ambassador to Japan, though he returned to lecture in various European countries. From 1927 to 1933 he was ambassador to the United States; then in 1933 to 1935 was ambassador to Brussels—an appointment that allowed him to travel throughout Belgium and Holland. From 1935 to his death in 1955, Claudel retired to his home in Brangues but often wintered in Paris. In 1946 he was elected to the French Academy, and in 1950 there was a poetic matinee devoted to him at the Vatican. Pius XII was present. When Claudel died on February 23, 1955, he was accorded a state funeral at Notre Dame de Paris. He was buried at Brangues.

During all of his years in successful, active diplomatic service, Claudel continued to write poetry, plays, letters, essays, and, especially in his retirement years, reflections and meditations on Holy

Scripture. In his more than sixty years of publishing, the basic elements of his works are Man, the World, and God. He explores the conflict between natural and supernatural forces. He saw the divine intervening in human lives and recognized the initiative taken by God. Claudel saw the *spiritual* human being and expressed the longing for eternal love. He said: "Amid all our vain preoccupations we are pursued by the feeling of emptiness which accompanies inactivity, unless we embrace the Cross, which stretches us to our fullest dimension."[10] A friend of Claudel's wrote: "From love to the Cross, and from the Cross to Resurrection and fulfillment: such is the direction and progression of Claudel's Catholicism."[11] For Claudel the world is a unity, a part of universal harmony, a drama in which something is happening at every instant of time. For him we are a part of it all. During his early searching, Claudel wrote: "I understand the harmony of the world; when will I grasp its melody?"[12] In the intellectual and political climate of his time Claudel was a nonconformist because he was not only an orthodox Catholic but also an author writing about his beliefs. Claudel said: "We must enter into the harmony of creation, counting ourselves as nothing; we have been placed on earth to write a story of God's choosing; our own story is of no interest."[13]

A friend characterized Claudel as both disciplined and free, a pioneer always open to progress, young in spirit, cheerful, and a born mimic who enjoyed singing. He was an enthusiastic hiker, and nature in all of its manifestations was a subject of endless fascination for him. He was kind and thoughtful, though sometimes gruff and surly. He loved little children; he was an educator. Claudel's extensive travels and wide experiences gave him a deep understanding of foreign civilizations and literature. As a result, he had a broad outlook on life and was deeply interested in world events.

Claudel went to daily Mass and then spent a quarter of, half of, or an entire hour in prayer, in conversation with God, daily. Of his hour of adoration he said: "I bring nothing and ask for nothing."[14] This man of shrewd intelligence loved solitude and silence, and throughout his life he was a seeker of God who lived his prayers and promises.

In *Letters to a Doubter*, Claudel states: "Where God is not, there can be no truth: where there is no being, there is nothing. But God is everywhere. He creates, sustains and contains all. We are the assistants at a continuous creation."[15]

Among the words offered at Claudel's burial were these: "[In Claudel], there was never a break between earthly reality and the mystery of God."[16] Claudel did not fear death. It was a door through which the seeker could enter to penetrate the mystery of the God for whom he longed all his life.

Paul Claudel epitomizes the words "seeker of God," which are at the core of Benedictine spirituality. This poet, dramatist, and diplomat could not accept the prevailing teachings of his time, which promoted a mechanical, random, materialistic view of life. He rejected this philosophy and his continued search for meaning led him through a spiritual struggle that was agonizing. Even after his mystical experience in Notre Dame Cathedral, and the resulting "I believe," Claudel continued the struggle to reconcile his faith with what had become his ingrained philosophy through his education and social climate. The opposition between his intellect and his intuitive sense of truth seemed irreconcilable for four years after he acknowledged God. During this battle to recover his faith completely and overcome his skepticism, Claudel read Blaise Pascal, Dante, Newman, and, above all, Scripture. He probed the Bible, allowed it to become central in his daily life and inspiration, and advised the "doubter" to read it from end to end. In this rootedness in Scripture, in his love of liturgy, the Divine Office, daily *lectio* and daily prayer, Claudel reveals and expresses a true Benedictine heart.

Claudel believed in a loving and personal God. He found human life to have deep, spiritual meaning with God's governing love as the foundation. His advice to a male nonbeliever asked the man to have an imperturbable faith in God's love; to try to spend at least a quarter of an hour each day on some sentence or story in the Gospel; to go to daily Mass if possible and follow the cycle of worship of the Catholic Church, and to practice works of active charity.

Claudel was a prominent figure in the French Catholic Renaissance of the early twentieth century. He was a prolific writer whose works convey artistic beauty and power, and he was a brilliant diplomat. He has been described as a mystic, enigmatic, mysterious, disciplined, cheerful, and sociable. His critics were many, but he was not deterred from what he believed to be truth. One cannot do justice to the man or his works in this short space. Suffice it to say that this Benedictine oblate is obviously a fine example of perseverance in the search for God and the meaning of life. He found God after doubts, fears, and many struggles, then continued to serve God faithfully to the very end of his life. In *Letters to a Doubter*, Claudel describes what every Benedictine would recognize as the vow of "conversion of morals" that she or he makes. Claudel says: "Conversions are always the result, not of some great pitched battle, but of a long series of little efforts carried to a successful conclusion."[17] Surely Benedict would agree.

Reflections and Insights on the Rule of Benedict

Oblate Esther de Waal, an Anglican scholar, writer, and laywoman, wrote that the Rule, for her, was neither remote, past, or cerebral but immediate and relevant, "speaking of things that I already half knew or was struggling to make sense of." She states:

> It tackled with honesty questions of personal relationships and authority and freedom; it recognized the need for stability and the need for change; it established a pattern for a balanced life; its sense of respect and reverence for people and for material things touched me immediately. I valued its insight on such day-to-day matters as hospitality or the attitude towards material possessions. Above all it spoke of a life that was essentially unheroic, much in fact like the life of any ordinary Christian family.[18]

Jane Tomaine, oblate and Episcopal priest, states that the Rule "fosters a way of life that is rooted and grounded in Christ, providing a tool to help us find a center of stability so needed in today's world."[19] She adds: "The Rule is very much about living an ordinary life well."[20] Tomaine quotes the Dutch Benedictine oblate, Will Derkse, who says:

> I have experienced that the Benedictine spirituality is a veritable treasure-trove of old and yet new insights which may be incarnated anew, concerning good leadership, informed decision-making, fruitful communication, good human re-

source management, salutary conflict resolution, a careful management of one's possessions, a blessed lifestyle which provides space. An attractive aspect is that Benedictine spirituality directs itself so distinctly toward what needs to be done here and now, at this moment.[21]

Sister Katherine Howard, OSB, states: "The *Rule* makes it plain that God is with us through and in Christ and the Holy Spirit in the daily events of life. Neither the poor nor the rich, the old nor the young, neither those in authority nor those subject to authority are excluded from the love of God. For God's presence to be effective in our life requires only our consent and cooperation."[22]

Joan Chittister, OSB, reminds us: "The Rule of Benedict is concerned with life: what it's about, what it demands, how to live it. And it has not failed a single generation."[23]

Roberta Bondi, an oblate of Saint Benedict's Monastery, Saint Joseph, Minnesota, says:

> With their love of God and each other, in their lives of prayer and work, in their commitment to a vision of society in which people truly flourish, in their freedom from social values and judgments that destroy or wilt the lives of women, in their extravagant hospitality, in their support of and pride in each other, I could see for myself that the sisters of St. Benedict's monastery really did embody what was best in the ancient monasticism that drew me.[24]

She adds: "I am convinced that Benedictine monasticism is a very significant resource both for the renewal of the universal body of Christ which is the whole Christian church, and for the modern world."[25]

Oblate Gerald W. Schlabach states: "In order to appropriate the Rule concretely, oblates might need to create fresh models by which to gather together as lay Benedictine 'base communities' dedicated to prayer, reflection, discernment, simplicity, peacemaking, and service." Reflecting on the Benedictine value/vow of stability, he states: "Inside or outside a monastery, it is of the very nature of stability that it opens us to God's presence in the ordinary. . . . Marriage, local church life, neighborhood life, good work, and better kinds of mobility when God does call us to move—all are opportunities to live out Benedictine stability, obedience and conversion of life in the world."[26]

In her book, *At Home in the World: A Rule of Life for the Rest of Us*, oblate Margaret Guenther, also an Episcopal priest, spiritual director, and retreat leader, writes: "Benedict's Rule deserves its popularity, especially among those of us who are trying to find our way in a complex and overstimulated world."[27] Addressing the Benedictine value/vow of stability, she quotes Anthony Bloom: "You will find stability at the moment when you discover that God is everywhere, that you do not need to seek Him elsewhere, that He is here."[28] She declares: "We too can experience a Benedictine stability, even as we live amid the changes and the chances of the world. This calls for perseverance, for holding on and hanging in, for making thoughtful choices and staying with them."[29]

Oblate Eric Dean—professor, layman, husband, parent, Presbyterian minister—says: "The *Rule* can speak to us of values that, even apart from the daily structures of monastic life, are relevant to our own lives in 'the outside world.'"[30] He continues: "St. Benedict speaks as a confrere of others who seek to be on their way to the heavenly city. Yet an authority rings through his words—the kind of authority our generation longs for even as it seeks to deny the domination that comes from power."[31] Saint Benedict calls us "daily to translate into action . . . [the Lord's] holy teachings."[32] Dean points out that "throughout the *Rule*, St. Benedict's ideas are marked by a particular sensitivity to personal feelings"[33] and that "the *Rule's* demands are frequently constructed in recognition of human fallibility and human needs."[34] In addressing the fact of our overstimulated lives, Dean says: "St. Benedict has caused us to reflect upon the fact that as the psalms call us to come to terms with ourselves as creatures before God, so prayer and silence teach us to avoid the kinds of stimulation that are themselves an avoidance of genuine personhood."[35]

The Rule of Benedict is not a legalistic document. "St. Benedict writes as though speaking in a personal way to a fellow Christian who is seeking God in the context of monasticism."[36] "St. Benedict's words strike home wherever men and women truly seek God in a spirit of simplicity and integrity."[37] Patrick Barry continues: "The spiritual emptiness that goes with overactivity and overachievement is being filled for many today in lay life through the wisdom of St. Benedict, which is ever old and ever new. . . . What appeals to the laity . . . is a beauty which is embedded in the center and radiates from Christ himself."[38] "It is the love of Christ and that love's power for healing and for leading us from darkness and death to eternal life that draws men and women toward Benedict's vision today."[39]

Benedict's Rule contains topics which deal with fundamental issues of life: our creaturehood, individuality, community, humility, forgiveness, discipline, leadership, understanding, prayer, love of God and neighbor, and more. What greater relevance to our lives could one ask for?

The spiritual inspiration and encouragement contained in the Rule are presented by Saint Benedict, a man steeped in Scripture, in such a way as to convey a sense of his companioning authenticity, his lived truth regarding our search for God and the meaning of life. Benedict reflects "in great depth on our relationship with our creator, our redeemer, on our use of the world we live in, on our interaction with each other, on our considered assessment of ourselves and our place in the universe, on freedom from vice and egomania, on our search for a peace and a fulfillment which is free from arrogance, greed, anger and all that disturbs the inner tranquility of 'the love of God which in its fullness casts out all fear.'"[40]

Oblate Dwight Longenecker, who is a husband and father, notes that the Rule can apply to family life by teaching us to employ the monastic sense of mutual obedience. It reminds us to listen to and obey God, as well as to listen to the needs of our children, typically manifested in their actions and unspoken communication. Each child is a unique individual with a unique blend of needs, gifts, and insights. According to Longenecker, Benedict teaches us to work with our children to discover the most complete fulfillment of God's will in their lives. Longenecker feels that just as the monks had to find God in the nitty-gritty of sixth century life, he is called to find God now, in the daily sacrifices, pressures, and uncertainties of family life of the twenty-first century. Longenecker also suggests that the "combination of liturgical prayer and spontaneous prayer works perfectly in the family life."[41] This aids in teaching the children that God is always with them and that they can turn to God at any time.

De Waal has written some classic texts on Benedictine spirituality. As a wife, mother, and seeker of God, she articulates beautifully not only what the Rule is about but how it applies to her life as a laywoman. In her article in *The Benedictine Handbook*, she says: "The Rule is like the Gospel itself, a spring or source to which one returns all the time, for it possesses a dynamism capable of inspiring the lives of those in every age who approach it prayerfully with openness and receptivity."[42] De Waal discovered how Benedict wants our lives to be "permeated with Christ." She has found that in our overly busy society we can lose a sense of balance and order which our application of the Rule could help remedy, since with Benedict there is no separation between praying and living. De Waal shares her perceptions of how Benedict respects the needs of the physical self; how he asks us to use our minds, talents, and artistic gifts and to rejoice in being human while living with attentiveness and openness to God's will, to the new, to the stranger. She also is impressed by the Rule's reminders to handle material things with respect and reverence, and she sees in this three implications: (1) for sharing our material things/gifts, (2) for environmental concerns, and (3) for working for social and racial justice. De Waal articulates many more insights and among them appreciates Benedict's knowledge about the demands of living with others and his wisdom in accepting, working with, and loving individuals without trying to control them.[43]

Rachel Srubas, a Presbyterian minister and oblate of Saint Benedict, finds that: "Much in the Rule, ancient though it is, pertains to the contemporary spiritual practices of prayer, humility, study, work, hospitality and simplicity."[44] She continues: "Many contemporary people of faith are drawn to Benedict because his teachings not only offer an antidote to the culture of overwork, they also promote an approach to sacred reading that engages the whole person, and not only the rational intellect."[45] She believes that "community—comprised of belonging, relationship and service—is the experience for which . . . many contemporary spiritual seekers yearn. It's through the community experience of work and worship, play and prayer that unconnected individuals become united in the knowledge that they are loved by the God of Jesus, and commit to living in Christ's name."[46]

The fact is that Saint Benedict lived at a time of chaos, turbulence, upheaval, confusion. Where was life's meaning? What values could give one an anchor? Today we face many of the same questions, and Benedict's solution, his Rule, can help us make sense of the fast-paced, disorderly jumble of daily living. What Benedict has to say is both relevant and profound. If followed, it can bring order and peace to those who live a chaotic life.

Lonni Pratt and Daniel Homan, OSB, in commenting on the Rule of Benedict remark that "each of us, if we are to survive with some self-respect intact, if we are going to sustain our ability to love, trust, and give, will need to find shelter for our battered souls."[47] They ask: "How do we stay tender in such a tough world? How do we remain true? How do we continue to feel? How do we keep getting up morning after morning and putting one foot in front of the other?" They maintain that living the Rule of Benedict—and the Gospel of Jesus on which it stands "will help us become people who are more open to others. We will become people who are fortified for the hard times and who can remain tender when we have to get tough. We will become people who have the courage to love, even though Jesus showed us that loving will be costly and put our lives at risk. We will become people who cease to fear the risk and are no longer easily shaken."[48]

Norvene Vest, in *No Moment Too Small*, shares: "The Rule coaxed and invited me, not to abandon all, but rather to embrace all, even while offering it daily back to God."[49] She has found the Benedictine way to healing and humanizing and discovered that Benedict asks "an attentiveness to what we are given in each day's experience" because "the specific problems we find hard in daily life can become a means of receiving God."[50] She also finds that, with Benedict, "no moment is too small for nearness to God."[51] Vest has come to realize that Benedictine spirituality teaches that God is involved in her life no matter what the circumstances and tells her how she can respond to God's presence in the here and now. The way Benedict addresses ordinary life and practical matters can be applied to our time. Our routines are filled with God's presence. "In response to an irate demand, can we speak lovingly? . . . When we begin a new task, do we depend entirely on our own strength or do we ask God's help? Are we sufficiently sensitive to the needs of others . . . ?"[52] Vest continues: "Benedictine spirituality is rooted in a movement from hearing to response to transformation . . . founded in silence, holy reading and prayer."[53] She reiterates again and again the fact that the Benedictine way offers a balanced way of life to those who seek God but are distracted by the problems and duties of everyday living. She concludes: "Benedict can reveal a way for us of focusing on the good, the true, and the beautiful, while his Rule teaches us how to work in cooperation with the realm of God always breaking into human history."[54]

These general testimonies about the Rule, how it can be lived, and how oblates live it, invite more specific attention to the document itself.

Selected Contemporary Interpretations of the Rule of Benedict

It is important that one does not look upon the Rule of Benedict in a legalistic sense. It is really a plan—a wonderful guideline that helps one to live a balanced life. It is a document full of wisdom and insights that helps us to understand how to live, love, become authentic, and attain peace. "Read it [the *Rule*] as you would good poetry or allegory. Mine it for depth of imagery; think about how the words written by Benedict might apply to a different time and situation."[55]

Vest reminds us that "the power of the Rule will increase when we can begin to encounter old words as if they were new, letting Benedict's different understanding gradually sink in and form our responses. We may discover something that helps us deepen our awareness of what is going on in our lives. We may find new vitality in familiar practices and discover that old, comfortable expressions of faith become stimulating encounters with God."[56]

"Behind the Rule lies Benedict's understanding of the purpose and quality of human life. Why are we created at all? What is the optimum relationship between human beings and the created world, and between human beings and God?"[57]

De Waal says: "One way of looking at the Rule is to see it simply as a handbook to making the very radical demands of the Gospel a practical, and therefore inescapable, reality in my daily life."[58] She sees the Rule as wisdom, not law—as a way of life and not a set of directives—something that gives her support as she journeys in her God-search.[59] De Waal assures us that Benedict is more concerned with why and how things are done, with the motivation behind an action, than he is with external conformity.[60] Benedict's Rule speaks to the heart because of his respect for persons and his confirmed knowledge of the mystery and assurance of God's grace working in each one.

David Steindl-Rast describes the Rule as a way to "put ourselves into a frame of mind that will lead us to live life in its fullness."[61] De Waal says: "It [the Rule] is all about love. It points me to Christ. Ultimately the whole meaning and purpose of the Rule is simply [in Benedict's own words], 'Prefer nothing to the love of Christ.'"[62] Read the Rule as an aid to living the Gospel and following Christ. Benedict was formed by the Word of God and the Rule abounds with scriptural content. Christ stands at the center.

The Rule of Benedict "is written for people with deeply spiritual sensibilities and deeply serious concerns who have no intention of setting out to escape their worlds but only to infuse their moral lights with the vision of the Divine."[63]

Benedict's Rule has demonstrated its flexibility, its adaptability, throughout centuries. It does not define and enforce boundaries but operates at the level of beliefs and values.[64] In his discussion on monastic life, Michael Casey, a well-known monk, author, and lecturer, asserts that Benedict established a dialectic "in which opposed but connected values act together to maintain direction in the midst of external change. It is this interaction that has ensured the survival of the Benedictine way of life."[65] Casey goes on to address the Benedictine charism by examining the areas of checks and balances, such as the fact that *conversatio* is tailored to fit persons, that distribution is made according to need, and that Benedict recognizes the existence of different gifts of grace.[66]

In "Living the Rule in the World" in *The Benedictine Handbook*, de Waal reminds us that in our overly busy world that applauds workaholics, Benedict shows us a life of balance and order in which there is no separation between praying and living. She reiterates that the Rule continues to call us to a life pattern of wholeness and balance. De Waal sees the Rule as countercultural, calling us to stay open to new ideas and questions, to become a disciple who will go on learning throughout a lifetime.[67]

Benedict wants us to be permeated with Christ, to become Christ-like. For Benedict, God is truly the beginning and the all of life. Since this is basically what being a Christian is about (and since most Christians live in community), the Rule, which is the result of Benedict's lived experience, is really for all. If we can read it in a slow, prayerful way, mindful of God's presence and with an openness to God's Spirit, it can help to form us. It is a Gospel-based plan for living that can address our needs at any stage of our life journey and help us develop and grow into who God intends us to be. The key point, however, as Benedict reminds us, is that we must truly seek God.

CHAPTER 3

Benedictine Life Gifts/Values for Oblates

Prefer Nothing to Christ (RB 72)

Benedict's mandate that one should value nothing whatsoever above Christ himself is basically the foundation of all that he hopes for us in writing his Rule. By cultivating the habit of living in the presence of God right now, daily, we are bringing together, learning to unite the *now* and the *daily* with the God of the promise who is already present. "In the world one is also in God, and when handling things one is also present to the Creator of all things."[1] Preferring nothing to Christ will also mean listening for God and to God in our prayer, *lectio*, and everyday experiences and then choosing the appropriate action in accord with the God-inspired insight, rather than following our own personal desires.

Reflection:

1. Why is it important to live in the present moment? How would doing so affect your peace of mind? Your level of stress?

2. God has created you and is sustaining your being every moment of your life. How can you arrange your day so that you never forget that truth?

3. Find a quiet place; sit in the stillness; close your eyes. Tell God you are here, ready to tune your ears to whatever message God chooses to give.

4. Thank God for all your blessings. Add God's strength to yours to overcome your struggles.

Seek God Daily

Seeking God is clearly related to preferring nothing to Christ. It is a quest that leads to consistent efforts to find God in everyday situations, experiences, and people with whom we associate. It is an effort to live in God's presence, to become aware of how God works in our lives, to become like Christ in our thoughts, words, and behavior. Seeking God is foundational to the monastic vocation and is the cornerstone on which Benedictine spirituality is built. (RB 58.7: "The concern must be whether the novice truly seeks God.") Seeking God is a lifelong journey for the longing human heart and continues whether at prayer, reading, or work, and whether in silence or relating in community. The implication in Benedict's way of seeking God is that we will find God in the present moment and in the people and life around us. He expects us to listen and stay alert so we don't miss God in the daily. As we seek this God daily and find him/her we grow in self-knowledge as well. Eventually the ultimate goal is then reached: growth into a deeper love of Christ and transformation into a Christlike presence/person.

Reflection:

1. Deep within each human is a longing that only God can satisfy. In our innermost being we know that there has to be more to life and that we need this "more" to be satisfied and at peace. Stop and think about this truth, relating it to your life and experiences.

2. Try to find God daily in the tedium or joy of the day, in your job, and in those with whom you interact. Were you really treated unjustly or just thought you were? Was there some catastrophe or some unexpected delight? Can you find God in it? God's message? How can you grow spiritually from whatever happens to you each day?

Conversion of Heart

Conversion is always a call to change, growth, development. Conversion is a vow for the Benedictine monastic, a call to change attitudes and behaviors into those more closely aligned with Christ. Though it is not a vow for oblates, it is a Benedictine gift and value for living. To be able to change implies an openness of mind and heart, even an openness to change, so we can be what God calls us to be. This implies a constant letting go, which, of course, is difficult. It calls for a nonjudgmental accepting of others with whom we live, work, socialize. It means that we must accept ourselves with all our foibles, tendencies, needs, and faults as well as talents, virtues, and graces. It means that after any failure we try again to listen to God—through prayer, Scripture, our experiences and associates—to begin anew, to change whatever in our lives leads away from God. Benedictine spirituality offers a support system for our efforts at conversion. Among these aids are: practicing the presence of God, keeping death always before our eyes, and utilizing Benedict's tools for good works.

We must live in the present moment, making sure that our deepest inner self and our external self are in harmony. Benedict asks us to continually strive to become authentic, fully human. He feels that an awareness of death is facing reality and will keep us on the road of conversion as it reminds us that we only have so many days in which to live, serve, become, and love.

Reflection:

1. Benedict's "Tools for Good Works" (RB 4) is loaded with texts right out of Scripture. It is strongly based on the Ten Commandments and is a compendium of how to grow spiritually. Are you able to live this: "Never do to another what you do not want done to yourself?" Try to imagine what the world would be like if each of us followed that principle daily.

2. Psychologists today would agree with Benedict's advice not to nurse a grudge. Did Benedict know that those who nurse resentments only harm themselves? Take a moment today to erase a hurt from your heart.

3. Benedict wants each person in his community to be a leaven for good. He asks that you aid the poor, visit the sick, help the troubled, support and console the grieving (those in sorrow / the sorrowful). Where have you had an opportunity to

make a positive difference in someone's life today? Did you recognize it and act on it?

Stability and Fidelity

For the monastic, stability is closely related to obedience and conversion of life. Stability is an aid to those who seek to persevere in their search for God. It is a confirmation of their commitment to seek God within a particular community with a specific group of people. It is a sign of their psychological and spiritual rootedness and closely related to a sense of who they are. For the oblate, as for the monastic, stability relates to being grounded in the where and the now. Stability means that I will persevere and endure; that I am at home with who I am and where I am and will cease my restlessness and wandering. I am alert and fully alive, ready to meet God where I am, knowing that God is faithful. Once I am at home with myself I can more easily move forward into the transformation called for by *conversatio*.

Be stable. "Do not be daunted immediately by fear and run away from the road that leads to salvation. It is bound to be narrow at the outset" (RB Prol. 48). Stability requires a certain tenacity, a courage to stay where one is amidst all the doubts and darkness. It is a commitment, a fidelity, and a trust that when we hold fast, God will be found.

Today, in our excessively mobile, overly flexible, continually restless lives and culture, the Benedictine concept of stability can act as an anchor, can help us hold fast to our principles, values, and commitments, as well as relational and even geographical ties. It can help us stay "home" in the midst of chaos.

An oblate's monastic community conveys even a sense of geographic security in a world where so much is continuous movement. For both monastic and oblates, *stability* means fixing one's heart on the Rock who is Christ and remaining faithful and steadfast where and with whom God has given us. Benedictine stability/fidelity advises us to stay in the reality of where we are placed and face our inner self and others with openness, faith, and a strong, wholehearted commitment to God.

Reflection:

1. It is not easy to hold to one's principles when the easiest way is to "give in." Make a list of what you consider your greatest life values. Are you really living them or are they constantly compromised? How?

2. Why do many people run from commitment? Is it the fear of being boxed in, disappointed, unable to fulfill the promise? What are the positives of fidelity to commitments?

3. Are you at home with who you are? If not, why not? Take stock of anything that impedes your ability to like yourself, to be alone, to be free of fear and fully alive.

4. Identify a "darkness" in your life. Address it with courage. Bring it into the light and see what solutions you can find to change it.

Listening and Loving Obedience

"We must, then, prepare our hearts and bodies for the battle of holy obedience to his instructions. What is not possible to us by nature, let us ask the Lord to supply by the help of his grace" (RB Prol. 40-41).

Cyprian Smith, OSB, believes that obedience is an indispensable ingredient in all relations and that "the essence of obedience is putting others before myself."[2] For Benedict, obedience is selflessness, the good of the other, and love, with its generous giving. He wants us to obey out of love for God. Benedict wants Benedictines to think of the needs of others rather than their own. Doesn't our own experience tell us that if there really is *mutual* consideration, one's dignity or rights will not be trampled on?

If we are to "put on Christ," obedience will no doubt play a part in our transformation. If we are serious about becoming "other Christs," if Christ is to act in and through us, there will have to be a releasing on our part of some of our autonomy. It is never easy to say or live "Thy will be done," but if one is serious about living life on the deepest spiritual plane, of becoming one with God in mind and heart, then God will become the controller of our lives. We are back to the word "openness," openness to God as God speaks to us through Scripture, *lectio divina*, and the promptings of the Holy Spirit through and in our lived experiences.

Letting go of our own desires is not easy nor does this attitude imply losing the essence of who we are or obeying others who demand immoral behavior. It does imply that when the required deed is neutral or good in itself we can perform it, even against our *natural* inclination, because we believe that God can and will work through the situation/action/acceptance. Obedience for Benedict means letting God and service in love to others be the motivating factors of our actions. Smith believes that such behavior will not negate our true and deepest self because we have chosen to align our will with God's, which leads to true freedom.[3]

Today's society does not like the word "obedience." People see it in a negative light because they focus on the concept of outside control, loss of independence and autonomy and even oppression or abuse. This is not the kind of obedience of which Benedict speaks. All of us are tuned to the will of those we love. We give our children, our spouse, our friends, and our work what is needed, often acting against our own inclinations and desires. Benedict knows that if we want to become more like Christ we need to listen to the God within us, to the person who is (or can be) God's agent, to the daily experiences in which God manifests himself/herself, and to the Scriptures and *lectio* where we meet God in the Word and prayer. In all of this, Benedict would want us to balance our needs with those of others on our way to transformation in Christ.

Reflection:

1. Benedict's first words in the Prologue of his Rule are: "Listen carefully." He refers to attending with the ear of one's heart to the voice of our God. Sit in the quiet for a few moments. Choose an experience you had today and ponder how God spoke to you in that action, event, or person. *Listen.* Then speak to God about it in any way you choose.

2. God's love always and everywhere is a given or we would cease to *be*. Begin your day by opening up and out to God,

reminding yourself that God is with you now, in this present moment, and will be with you throughout your life. God is ready; always attentive and available to show love and support. Listen for and discern what God's will is for you as you live today and project into the future. When you discover it, tell God "yes" and you cannot go wrong.

3. God's love is unconditional. If we are to be Christlike we will strive for unconditional love. It is not easy for humans to reach that state because of our egos and selfish nature. If you can be a friend or find a friend who loves unconditionally, you are truly blessed and godlike. Try to love people as they are and not as you want them to be. Hard, isn't it?

Balancing Prayer and Work

"We believe that the divine presence is everywhere. . . . But beyond the least doubt we should believe this to be especially true when we celebrate the divine office" (RB 19.1-2). (This means the Liturgy of the Hours, and inclusively, all prayer.)

Benedictine prayer is Bible centered. "The Word, for Benedict, meant pre-eminently Christ, the divine Word speaking through the Bible and met in other people."[4]

Benedict asked his monks to devote about three hours a day to *lectio divina*, thus freeing them to meet God in sacred reading that led to prayer. Benedict saw *lectio* as an "opportunity for awareness of God's presence."[5] Perhaps one of the biggest challenges of our time is to free up a part of each day for God so that we can focus on God's word in the Bible and on other sacred literature, so that we can reflect on what the reading is saying to our minds and hearts, to see how God is asking us to apply the Word to our lives here and now. The message received can then weave its way throughout our day and help to nourish us in the midst of our hectic lives. Our reflection during *lectio*, and our conversation with God as a result of it, can act as a type of daily refreshment and spiritual renewal to counteract the frenetic pace of our lives and the clamor for attention that we meet in the excessive verbiage, hype, and noise-bombardment in our world.

Prayer is at the heart of not only Benedictine life but also Christian life. God is in me. God is at the center of who I am and what I am called to be. Prayer is a must if I am to connect with God, open myself up to my communion with God, deepen my relationship with God. If I seek to be God's instrument for good in this world, it is vital that I open my deepest self (my core) to the spiritual reality of God within me; try to remove the obstacles that prevent me from engagement with the divine reality whether these obstacles come from within or without. Prayer means giving our time to God in self-surrender. Whether we feel God's presence or not, we are there for God in openness, desire, attitude, and essence during the time we have set aside for prayer. We trust in God during our prayer time and we know that God always hears us no matter how we feel. Key words for the oblate in prayer are *trust, openness,* and *surrender* to an all-loving God with whom we want to deepen our relationship, our union. God is in charge.

De Waal sees Benedict's approach to prayer as trying to form in us an underlying attitude of total dependence on God, the constant awareness of God's presence, the demand of continual perseverance and patience, and above all the motivation of love. She says: "The whole of my life is to become prayer."[6]

Chittister reminds us that: "Prayer unmasks. Prayer converts. Prayer impels. Prayer sustains us on the way."[7]

Pratt considers that: "Prayer trains us to hear God's presence in our world, in all the people who silently walk into the rooms of our lives, and in all the words not spoken."[8] She believes that often it is our busyness that we blame for our failure to pray and that the antidote to that excuse is Benedict's suggestion to keep your prayer "short and pure" (RB 20.4-5)—i.e., *simple.* Pratt goes on to remind us that we can pray while walking, exercising, sitting still, or while in the car or shower.[9] Prayer will help us become increasingly aware of the God we long for and love.

In his Prologue Benedict says that "every time you begin a good work, you must first pray to [God] most earnestly to bring it to perfection" (RB Prol. 4). Benedict would also agree with Julian of Norwich that: "Prayer is profitable though you feel nothing, though you see nothing, yes, though you think you can do nothing. . . . [God] covets our continual prayer."[10]

The oblate's spiritual goal is union with God and it is fueled by consistent and daily prayer in order to connect to that God in all of life's experiences, relationships, and situations. This includes the realities of a life that tries to balance prayer and work.

For Benedict, idleness is an enemy of the soul (RB 48) and work is dignified, even holy. Work is using the talents God gave us, developing them, and giving them back to God through our service to others as we help to build God's kingdom here on earth. In Benedictine spirituality, work and prayer are partners. *Ora et labora* is a Benedictine motto.

For Benedict there is no sense of inferior work. All is necessary, all is valuable, and all should be done responsibly and with care, using the gifts that we are given. Moderation is important and we must balance work with prayer.

Benedict values the individual and recognizes the uniqueness of each person. In his knowledge of human nature he sees the importance of balancing things of the spirit and mind with those of the body. He provides that all individuals carry their share of the workload. In this way, the community is also built up while the individual lives in a holistic way. When Benedict exhorts us to pray so that our inner being is in harmony with our outer, external words, he is also giving us a model for work. We should be using the gifts God gave us in such a way that our work is an expression of who we are. While no one "job" will allow us to express all of our gifts or who we are, our hobbies or volunteer work can help us fill that need. The main point is to keep a rhythm in our days, weeks, lives, that will allow us to attend to all aspects of who we are: soul, mind, body. Each of us must commit ourselves to achieving a *balance* in our own life by assessing where we are and then acting to attain it. When we have arrived at a wholesome balance we are better equipped to serve others, whether it be in work, family, civic, or church communities or even globally.

Relative to this, Benedict would have us look at all material things as though they were "vessels of the altar" (RB 31.10). The idea is stewardship; it is taking care of what we are given, and that includes time, gifts, body, mind, and soul.

Reflection:

1. Can two people ever develop a relationship without conversing? How can we develop a relationship with God if we never think about God, open ourselves out to God's presence, listen to God, speak to God? Take just a few moments each day for prayer and your life could change.

2. Have you been praying to God and feeling nothing? That is where *trust* comes in. I have a theory that God is pleased with not only the effort but also the desire to pray. Don't let your feelings dictate whether or not to pray. Just be there with the desire, open out to God, and let God act.

3. You can pray anywhere, at any time. You do not need a formula or a method. Just *be* with God who is already there listening and waiting.

4. How do you feel about your job? Does it fulfill you; does it energize you? If not, stop a moment to reflect on why. Are you not motivated because your talents are not being used? Is it boring whereas you prefer a challenge? Do your coworkers irritate you? Why? Is it only your attitude you need to change or does the situation call for something more drastic?

5. Benedict respected the dignity of the worker and saw the dignity of all work. How do your job and work efforts contribute to the good of your family, your community, our world?

6. God sent his Holy Spirit to us to carry on the work Christ began. I once opened a religion class with these words: "Christ has no hands but yours; no eyes, ears, mouth but yours; no feet but yours to carry Him to others wherever you go. *You* are now Christ on earth." The students looked at me with alarm yet fascination, as they absorbed the message. How will you be Christ today?

7. Whatever work you do, think of yourself as being a cocreator with the God who gave you life and all your talents. Try to remain centered on God during your work; listen to God as you do it; seek God in the doing.

8. Can idleness day after day give one a sense of self-worth and fulfillment?

9. You are unique in all the world. No one exactly like you has ever lived. Assess where you are in the use of your talents and in balancing your life of work with that of prayer. How can you live in a holistic way? Benedict's knowledge of human nature points the way.

Community

"The workshop where we toil faithfully . . . is the enclosure of the monastery and stability in the community" (RB 4.78).

Each monastery is basically a family, a community of believers, rooted in geographical and spiritual place, with a commitment to seek God together.

Benedict knew that each individual is at a certain stage of spiritual development and that living together in daily contact meant that at times there would be a strain in interpersonal relationships. He deals with those aspects of communal life by calling us forth to Christian love and forgiveness as well as mutual obedience and a sense of personal responsibility. While relationships provide challenges, they are also a means to personal growth. While contemporary cultures value individualism (which may result in alienation, even isolation), Benedictine spirituality recognizes that we humans do not operate in a vacuum and that what we do and say affects other people.

"This, then, is the good zeal which monks must foster with fervent love: *They should each try to be the first to show respect to the other* (Rom 12:10), supporting with the greatest patience one another's weakness of body or behavior. . . . No one is to pursue what he judges better for himself but, instead, what he judges better for someone else" (RB 72.3-7.)

What a contrast to our prevailing individualism! Community for Benedict meant mutual giving, support, respect, love, in union with and focused in God. Benedict knew that if real community was to be formed, the selfishness that can accrue from preoccupation with "number 1" (myself) would be negated through relationships developed while living together as a family with Christ at the center and God as the priority in life. When we look outward to the other and even toward eternity, we are not navel gazing but are rather all about being a God-like presence for our families, parishes, cities, and world. As we give of ourselves we start to develop and fulfill our own personal potential as well as helping others become what God meant them to be. We have continually seen how *equality* is a key word in Benedictine spirituality where even the young are listened to, where each is concerned for the other's welfare regardless of that person's age, function, or gifts, and where everyone takes a turn at community tasks. It is in our human relationships and our lives in community that we can begin to discover our own rough edges, our own personal areas that need redemption. Then we can begin the psychological, emotional, and spiritual growth by giving of self to others in care and concern as did Christ. This life in community does not diminish us as unique individuals but helps us to develop into that irreplaceable, even holy, creation that God intended from our birth.

Oblates have their monastic community as well as their family and larger communities. Applying the Rule of Benedict to all will help to foster personal and communal spiritual growth. "To know God and others we must understand ourselves, but to know ourselves we must rely on the help of others."[11] The Rule of Benedict encourages self-awareness and awareness of others, all in relationship and rooted in God.

Reflection:

1. We read that in today's society people hunger for community. Benedictine spirituality stresses the importance of life in community. While Benedict is careful to recognize the uniqueness of each member and treats him or her accordingly, he also knows that in order to grow to maturity one has to be involved with other humans in relationship. Being with others and interacting with them helps us to define who we are. Choose a personal relationship in your life and try to follow what traits of yours it brings to light. How did it help you discover who you are, what you think, how you respond to events?

2. What were the dynamics of the family in which you were raised? How did living in that community affect who you are today?

3. Name the communities to which you belong (civic, church, workplace, etc.). Choose one and list the pluses and minuses of your membership in it. Has it contributed to your personal growth spiritually, emotionally, psychologically?

4. Would you be a different person with different personality traits, character traits, developed talents and strengths if you had chosen to join a different set of communities?

5. How does living Benedict's advice to be the first to show respect to the other—to be patient with each other's weaknesses of body or behavior—assist an individual's spiritual and emotional growth?

6. How do you respond to unjust and false accusations, judgments, and gossip about you? Can this aspect of living in your specific communities help you to grow spiritually? How do you, or how would you, handle it?

Hospitality

"All guests who present themselves are to be welcomed as Christ, for he himself will say: *I was a stranger and you welcomed me* (Matt 25:35). Proper honor must be shown to all, *especially to those who share our faith* (Gal 6:10) and to pilgrims. . . . Great care and concern are to be shown in receiving poor people and pilgrims, because in them more particularly Christ is received" (RB 53.1-2, 15).

Pratt quotes a friend as saying that hospitality is "making room inside yourself for another person."[12] Who needs attention, kindness, graciousness where you live, where you work? Accept them as they are, welcome them into your presence, show them your concern, treat them as you would treat the incarnated Christ in your midst. Note how this sense of hospitality is related to Benedict's efforts to keep us open to the moment and God's presence in it. In that stance we are also to be Christ *for* others, *to* others.

As we go through each day and encounter the constant throngs of people, we note the frantic activity, the supersocializing, and we can become drained to the point of exhaustion. If we ourselves are overextended, we may need to start being hospitable to ourselves. We may need to take time, as Christ did, to refuel our energy so that we can again become a welcoming presence and receive the stranger with warmth, respect, and genuine charity. While Benedict legislates for hospitality to the stranger and the guest, he reminds his followers that they must also show respect and honor to those with whom they live. For oblates that means family, coworkers, fellow travelers, parishioners—all with whom we have relational contacts. Recall that Benedict calls for mutual obedience, equality, acceptance, listening, mutual love, and openness to one another in various parts of his Rule. All of this and more is applicable to the hospitality he seeks to develop *within* the monastery and with respect to strangers. No doubt Benedict hoped that this ripple of Christlike behavior would spread beyond the monastery walls to eventually touch a needy world. Wherever monastics are, wherever oblates are, we must continue to ask at the end of each day as we reflect on our contacts: "Did we see Christ in them? Did they see Christ in us?"[13]

As we practice Benedictine hospitality we may not be surprised to find that "it is the first step toward dismantling the barriers of the world."[14]

Reflection:

1. Benedict mandates that all guests at the monastery should be received like or as Christ. Perhaps that is easiest when they are expected and did not unexpectedly interrupt one's plans. Reflect on how you respond to the sudden interruption of your schedule by people who show up without warning or invitation. Would you respond differently if you saw them as Christ in person? Ponder how.

2. How do you respond to the poor and homeless in our society? Do you think: "She could get a job if she wanted to. She is just lazy." Are you able to stay open to the possibility that the person you encountered has tried all avenues for help and has

failed? Can you still respect that person, reach out to her and even make the small effort of a kind word in passing? Try it and see what it does for you.

3. Are you able to do volunteer work at church, a nursing home, a hospital, any place that will allow you to be a Christlike presence for the needy?

4. Can you see Christ in the people affected by negative societal issues whether in this country or abroad? Can you do your best to be an advocate for them by taking the problem to your legislators and supporting positive action on behalf of those needy?

5. Benedict would also want you to be hospitable to yourself. Do you eat right, get enough sleep, share your troubles with friends? Do you set aside some time each day to enrich yourself through quiet and prayer? Do you read enriching books, engage in a preferred hobby? The more wholesome you are, the more genuinely hospitable you can be.

Humility

The twelve degrees of humility that Benedict gives us are a great reminder that the world does not revolve around us and that God is in charge. Humility is basically acknowledging and accepting the truth about things, ourselves, others, reality. Being humble is not the same as being humiliated or enjoying humiliation. Neither is it negating our talents or gifts. Our society often invites us to make ourselves gods or to idolize power, material things, prestige. If we are humble we are aware that we are not the center of the universe, and that we have no business trying to lord it over, dominate, or control others. Benedict reminds us that we should always have the fear of God before our eyes, be mindful of God's commands, accept the will of God as it appears in our life—even accepting it through obedience to others whom God has given to direct us. He reminds us that often life is not easy and we must be patient when we encounter difficulties. We must persevere despite aggravations and unjust treatment. We must keep trying and "*when pressed into service for one mile, they go two* (Matt 5:39-41)" (RB 7.42).

Benedict wants us to be honest about who we are so he asks us to admit our faults and offenses. Since that requires self-awareness and sharing who we really are, we actually are applying what today's psychologists would consider a tool for good mental health.

As we continue to explore the steps of humility we find that Benedict asks us to be content with what we really need, to stay open to learning about life, to control our tongue and be gentle in speech, and show, even in our bearing/mien that we have others, ourselves, and God in clear perspective. In Benedict's humility, we do not lose personal dignity or the fact that we are God's beloved. We merely remember that we are the creature and not the Creator and try to act accordingly. This may be countercultural, but it is not demeaning. It is freeing.

Reflection:

1. Benedict's twelve steps of humility will not be popular with anyone who thinks that the steps are meant as a negation, debasement, demeaning of the human being. If you read this chapter (RB 7) in the Rule, you must remember to relate the text to its time. Once again Benedict leans on Scripture. He suggests that we must be vigilant and serious in our desire to seek God. God knows our every desire. After all, God created us and keeps us in being. Humility on our part will recognize that, acknowledge it as true, and reject the fallacy that we are all and the center of all. That in no way reduces our importance or value as a human being. It merely helps us to keep things in perspective by reminding us that we are not God.

2. It is a part of humility to admit that we are not in control. There is suffering in our life and often we cannot alleviate it or even understand the "why" of it. At that point we must enter into the mystery of suffering, talk to God about it, and endure it with God's help. Benedict would consider that humility. Stop for a moment and identify a situation, person, or thing that causes or has caused you suffering in your life. Are you tested as intensely as Christ was on Calvary? Christ

was obedient unto death. The humble person will remember that we are greatly loved by God and will trust God in all the experiences of life. "Giving it to God" does help to make the burden lighter.

3. For Benedict, humility entails being honest about oneself. That means that arrogance and pride will have little place in an individual's life. We are to be aware that all are equal in God's eyes and act accordingly, not considering ourselves better than our neighbor. We will refrain from judging; from being insolent, overbearing, and tyrannizing to others, since we know we have a "beam" in our own eye.

4. All the steps of humility that Benedict states are intended to develop an authentic and habitually virtuous human being who will arrive at the love of God, which casts out all fear. Are you free enough of inner conflict to be able to persevere on the path to God? Can you persevere even through suffering and unjust treatment?

5. Remember this basic thought: humility is truth.

Silence

Humility can be related to so many aspects of the Rule such as the conversion of morals, obedience, hospitality, and community. It is a virtue that can lead one to a deep peace. While silence is not literally a virtue, it is a gift and value of Benedictine spirituality for our personal growth and for the calming counteraction it provides in our daily frenetic environment.

Benedict's chapter on restraint of speech (RB 6) is a reminder that not only should *evil* speech be curbed but also *good* words, at times. If we are to be truly good listeners; if we are to hear that Word among us; that ever-present God inside us, we must have silence. As we live our lives in this culture we are constantly bombarded with noise. Television and radios blare nonstop, cars whiz by, halls and elevators abound with music; iPods, earphones, smart phones, transistors give us music and news and talk shows; telephones put us on hold and spew intermittent messages to assure us how important our call is; pagers, ATVs, motorboats, Jet Skis, machines of all types announce their presence. Our ears and minds are assaulted all through the days and sometimes through the nights until noise becomes the norm even for children; until we become numb with the vibrations. While real silence is not easy to come by, could it be that many do not seek it because in silence we come face-to-face with who we really are, with "what life is about," with the fact of discomfort in our own skin and in our circumstances, relationships, spiritual life?

Benedict knew that we had to make time for silence in our lives so that we could hear and respond to God's voice within us and even to listen to God speaking through others and in the Word. Remember Elijah (1 Kgs 19:9-13): God was not in the whirlwind but in a sound like a whisper. God is also in our ordinary situations, in visitors, strangers. Silence helps us remember and maybe carry out in our daily lives the truth that God is present everywhere and in everything. "By practicing silence, we allow ourselves to be taught by God's presence."[15]

How can oblates begin to apply Benedict's recommendation for silence in their busy lives? Vest suggests taking an occasional coffee break alone; moving to the foyer or garden and sitting quietly for several minutes; driving home on a less crowded, less noisy route; walking alone in a park; spending a few days at a retreat center.[16] Each person can identify areas in his or her life that would offer an opportunity to develop silence, which in turn could improve the ability to really listen. When we have successfully found a place, space for exterior silence, we can more easily start to focus on the interior self. To achieve interior silence we will face ourselves, and through all the distractions offered by heart and mind, we will continue to be attentive to the God who is with us and in us. With *lectio*, prayer, and an interior silence that allows increasing awareness of the presence of God in other people and in our daily activities, we can help minister to an increasingly noisy and frantic society.

Smith suggests that the aching emptiness in peoples' hearts in this age of great achievements and technological advancements is manifested in the fear of silence.[17] The need of God, for God, is real but rarely recognized as such by our preoccupied world. If we want to grow spiritually, all of us need to cultivate exterior and interior silence.

Reflection:

1. Stop a moment to reflect if silence has played any role in your day. Did you seek asylum from the noise or was that silence an accidental gift? How long did the silence last and were you comfortable in it and grateful for it? If so, why? If not, why not?

2. How can you achieve a measure of *exterior* silence in your busy day? Is there a room to which you can go to shut out all noise? Could you stop by a church and sit quietly in God's presence for a time? How about visiting a library and finding a quiet nook? Try now to identify where you can find some *exterior* silence in your life. Bask in the quiet, breathe deeply, and just *be*.

3. Can you list any ways in which silence would allow you to develop your spiritual life?

Authenticity

The dictionary defines the word "authentic" as "conforming to fact and therefore worthy of trust, reliance or belief."[18] To put it another way, an authentic person is one who is genuine in the sense of "what you see is what you get." When one acts from the sense of who she or he really is, there is no artificiality, no need to dissemble, to prevaricate, to exaggerate, "to put on airs." One who is authentic is comfortable with who she or he is and can move through life with a sense of freedom and peace. How stressful and exhausting it must be to lie to oneself and carry around different personal masks to be adapted to each occasion as it occurs and to please others. If humility helps us to know and live the truth about who we are in relationship to God and creation; if silence helps us discover, ponder, and remember who we are in relationship to the temporariness of life, then authenticity is the result of consistently acting on the truths of self and creation as we know them.

Knowing and being our *true* selves, as God made us and loves us, will help us value, as did Benedict, our individuality and uniqueness. We won't need to embellish our successes or our identity. We will also be able to accept our failures as merely the result of being human and imperfect, and when we do fail, we will pick ourselves up and make further efforts to improve. We will view any failure as an opportunity for growth and improvement rather than a means of diminishment and self-loathing.

As authentic persons, we say what we mean and mean what we say. We put our energy into developing genuineness instead of into changing facades, and we offer to a world that needs disguises the open-faced genuineness of a human being in tune and in harmony with truth, self, creation, and Creator.

Authentic persons value individuality as gift and will respect the uniqueness and individuality of others. This can lead to nonjudgmental living, to acceptance and respect of others, and to a personal comfort level that keeps one attuned to the important things of life versus the artificial and superficial. It can help us to keep things in perspective. One can trust an authentic persons to say and do what they say they will. If they "tell it like it is," they will do so without aggressiveness or desire to offend because they respect truth, live in reality, and reverence others.

Accepting who I really am is not a license to embrace personal weaknesses as much as an invitation to recognize them, correct them, and move forward toward being the best self possible, evolving into that fullness of being, that wholeness and holiness, which God has desired and intended for each of us from the beginning of creation. Accepting who I really am does not negate the efforts at conversion, transformation, development into a better self. On the contrary, honest self-awareness is a solid starting point for true personal growth.

Authentic persons are honest about personal deficiencies as well as strengths and gifts. The effort to be true to who they really are will be an asset toward a self-knowledge that can lead to accepting others as they really are. Such an attitude/stance bodes well for relationships in family and other community settings. Honest self-knowledge and self-acceptance can be a plus in efforts to understand others. "We understand others when we understand ourselves."[19]

Benedict implies self-knowledge in so many aspects of the Rule, especially when addressing needs. Regarding distribution of goods he writes, "Whoever needs less should thank God and not be distressed, but whoever needs more should feel humble because of his weakness, not self-important because of the kindness shown him" (RB 34.3-4). Benedict calls the abbot to personal authenticity by reminding him to be a living example of what he preaches (RB 2.11-13). He calls the abbot to mindfulness of each monk's individuality, to awareness that he is serving a variety of temperaments and the fact that he must "accommodate and adapt himself to each one's character and intelligence" (RB 2.31-32). He reminds the abbot that he "must so arrange everything that the strong have something to yearn for and the weak nothing to run from" (RB 64.19)

In chapter 4, verse 62, Benedict advises: "Do not aspire to be called holy before you really are, but first be holy that you may more truly be called so." In chapter 19, verse 7, he says, "Let us stand to sing the psalms in such a way that our minds are in harmony with our voices." We will extend that to say, "Let us be our best selves and then let our actions follow out of who we truly are."

Reflection:

1. Have there been times in your life when you put on a false persona? Why did you do so and did it make you feel good about yourself or uncomfortable?

2. What are the reasons for your sometimes behaving as you really do not want to behave? Is it societal pressure? Wanting to be one of the group? Fear of being rejected if you let your true self be known?

3. How can valuing, accepting, and respecting your individuality lead to nonjudgmental living on your part?

4. What does Rolheiser mean when he says: "We understand others when we understand ourselves"?

5. Benedict's Rule shows that he recognized and valued each individual. He advises us to express personal needs; to have our minds in tune with our hearts—really, to be who we are.

Along with that we are to respect others as they are. Try to single out a person who has injured you or whom you find difficult to accept. Identify ways in which you can improve your ability to accept them.

Reverence and Respect

"This, then, is the good zeal which monks must foster with fervent love: *They should each try to be the first to show respect to the other* (Rom 12:10), supporting with the greatest patience one another's weaknesses of body or behavior, and earnestly competing in obedience to one another. No one is to pursue what he judges better for himself, but instead, what he judges better for someone else" (RB 72.3-7).

Benedict's Rule is sprinkled throughout with reminders of individual differences and the respect we owe ourselves and each other. "The abbot is to show equal love to everyone" (RB 2.22). "A man born free is not to be given higher rank than a slave" (RB 2.18). "Great care and concern are to be shown in receiving poor people and pilgrims, because in them more particularly Christ is received" (RB 53.15). "The younger monks, then, must respect their seniors, and the seniors must love their juniors" (RB 63.10). "It is written: *Distribution was made to each one as he had need* (Acts 4:35). By this we do not imply that there should be favoritism—God forbid—but rather consideration for weaknesses. Whoever needs less should thank God and not be distressed, but whoever needs more should feel humble because of his weakness, not self-important because of the kindness shown him" (RB 34.1-4).

Chapter 2, on the "Qualities of the Abbot," offers some specifics about individual differences, definite consideration of them, and how to accommodate them. At the basis of this respect for all—whether they are fellow monks young or old, or guests, strangers, slaves or free—is the truth that Benedict finds Christ in all persons. They are precious to God, they are precious to Benedict, they should be precious to all who call themselves monastics and/or Christians. Benedict recognizes that God created each person to be unique and that whenever people are living together, the strengths and weaknesses of each individual will become obvious. We are to love our personal uniqueness, accept our limitations, and continue to transform our lives to emulate Christ. Similarly, we are to accept others as they are and patiently help them activate their potential for growth and holiness no matter who they are, what skills they possess, or from where they originate. Once we realize and live the intrinsic dignity of each person and do not base our judgments or acceptance of them on their skills or talents, on their position in society and community, or on what they "do," we can start to form a solid foundation for mutual obedience and community. This goal of seeing Christ in all whom we meet daily, in accepting them as they are, is not easy to achieve. Obviously we will need great patience with ourselves and that can be acquired more readily by living in the present moment and by frequently reminding ourselves that it is God who has ultimate control of all things. We will be tested time and time again. A sense of perspective as well as humor could help us get through the tough times. A healthy love of ourselves and care for ourselves will also be a boon to achieving respect for those who constantly test our virtue.

While we are to respect and reverence *persons*, Benedict reminds us that material things also come from God and are "sacred vessels." The monastery cellarer is advised to "regard all utensils and goods of the monastery as sacred vessels of the altar" (RB 31.10). Thus Benedict presents us once more with an opportunity to see *all* created things as coming from God. The connections to stewardship, humility, authenticity, community living, and other Benedictine values treated here are obvious. All creatures and things are made by God and given to us as gifts. They are precious; *you* are precious. Live in gratitude, peace, and joy; grow and transform yourself with God's help into that special, unique human being that you were created to be. Use your gifts, find your joy in serving and loving others. Talk to God often in prayer and listen to God in the quiet of your heart and in the people and experiences of each day. Welcome the stranger, care for the sick, feed the hungry, live the Gospel. And above all, as Benedict advises, "Prefer nothing to Christ."

Reflection:

1. How would your world change if everyone you knew followed Benedict's advice to pursue what is judged better for someone else than what is better for yourself? Is this realistically possible?

2. How do you feel about Benedict's statement that if you need less you should thank God and not be perturbed, and that whoever needs more should feel humility rather than self-importance. Take stock of the needs in your life. Are they filled? Which needs are not met, and how can you change that?

3. If you see your neighbor having/receiving more of anything that you crave and have not, how do you handle the potential for jealousy, envy, and uncharitableness?

4. When people live together the strengths and weaknesses of each individual become more blatant. Identify a character, personality, or behavioral weakness of an individual with whom you live, work, or associate. How can you better learn to respect and accept that person?

5. Consistently try to see Christ in each person you meet, and when your efforts to do that are challenged, give it to God in prayer.

6. How do you use the material things you possess? Benedict suggests they are to be used as "sacred vessels of the altar." Clothes, dishes, furniture, cars—all creation comes from God. Do you care for all? If you need to improve in this area, where would you begin? Make it step-by-step, not all or nothing.

Joy

"But as we progress in this way of life and in faith, we shall run on the path of God's commandments, our hearts overflowing with the inexpressible delight of love" (RB Prol. 49).

The "delight," the happiness, to which Benedict refers in this passage is not that passing pleasure that may come from good companionship, relaxed vacation, good food, or the like. It is a gospel joy whose source is the good news of God's unconditional love for us. It is Christian joy, anchored in faith and trust in the living God. In that sense it is related to the peace that comes from knowing that God is always with us, present through pain and sorrow, present through dryness of spirit and depression, present through ecstatic experiences whether of body or mind.

Benedictine spirituality is scriptural and living it means hearing and praying words such as: "Do not be afraid; you are of more value than many sparrows" (Luke 12:7). "Rejoice in the Lord always; again I will say, Rejoice" (Phil 4:4). "I have said these things to you so that my joy may be in you, and that your joy may be complete" (John 15:11). Benedictine spirituality means frequently praying with the psalmist words such as these: "In your presence there is fullness of joy" (Ps 16:11), "shout for joy, all you upright in heart" (Ps 32:11), "in the shadow of your wings I sing for joy" (Ps 63:7), "at the works of your hands I sing for joy" (Ps 92:4).

Living Benedictine spirituality means being aware of God's presence in myself. If God loves me unconditionally I must be precious. If Jesus, God's only Son, died for me, I have inestimable value. Knowing that, I can accept myself as I am, open my eyes to what is the best in me and to ways I can improve, and try to move closer to God, to become more like the God who loves me. What a source of joy! I don't have to be anyone but myself. All the pressures to pretend and prevaricate, all the reasons to worry and fear are gone.

That isn't all the good news. There's more! God is not only in me but also in my neighbor and in the ordinary circumstances/ experiences of daily life. When we go out to serve others, to give of ourselves, Christian joy is right around the corner. When we have learned how to forgive and tried to forgive ourselves and our neighbor, we can let go of guilt and bitterness. When we reach out to serve those in need there is no room for boredom. When we leave the past in the hands of our all-loving God, when we recognize the future as mere potential and out of our control, we can receive one of God's and Benedict's greatest gifts: the reminder and ability to *live* in the *present* moment with our God who loves us unconditionally. This can be a type of prayer in which we acknowledge that God is in charge and "all will be well." What daily joy and peace such an attitude, truth, reality brings! *It will help us to live totally in our God* who *is* Love, Joy, and Peace.

While we stay open to God's spirit in the present and give ourselves to God in our prayers, daily good deeds, efforts at spiritual growth, we can also connect with God concretely in the Eucharist. What a source of joy: the coming of Jesus Christ into the world to share our humanity; his resurrection that conquered sin and death for all time and opened the gates of heaven; his loving gift of self in Communion. These truths reflect on the chief reason for all joy: God's unconditional love for each of us. I repeat it so often because it is easily verbalized but seemingly less able to be realized. When we *do* live that realization and return God's love, inexplicable joy awaits. As Saint John Vianney said: "It is always springtime in the heart that loves God." Benedict knew that and lived that. He invites us to do the same.

Reflection:

1. Do you really believe that God loves you unconditionally? It is not easy to love at all, but the fact of God's faithful love should give you a sense of security, peace, and quiet joy that no one can take from you. Stop a moment and ponder God's unconditional love. Then express your joy in the special way you choose.

2. To love unconditionally is almost impossible for humans because of our innate tendency to selfishness. If you have a parent, spouse, or friend who loves you unconditionally you have received one of God's greatest gifts. Thank God for it daily and remind your family/friend of the preciousness of that love and of how you treasure it.

3. Giving your time, energy, help, material goods to others can bring you a joy that is of God. Try reaching out to the needy and be God's love for them. The needy could be your own family, a neighbor, a friend, a complete stranger. Identify them; give to them in some way and start to know the joy of God.

Peace

One who has achieved a type of interior silence is certainly on the way to the Benedictine value of peace. The experience of inner peace, the result of living continually in the awareness of the presence of Christ and life *in* Christ, can be the oblate's gift to the tension and stress in relationships, in the workplace, and in the community of believers and nonbelievers.

In the Prologue to his Rule, Benedict urges us to pursue peace as a goal (RB Prol. 17). See also chapter 4, verses 70-74: "If you have a disagreement with someone, make peace with him before the sun goes down." Benedict knew that being a peacemaker requires of the individual an inner peace, which, in turn, is acquired through prayer and union with God's will as perceived in self, circumstances, and others. To heal, to forgive, and to reconcile are some of the qualities needed for the peacemaker. To achieve peace in the family we must recognize the needs of self and others and try to see that they are met within reason. We must know ourselves and try to know and accept others. Benedict did not want grumbling or murmuring in his community. He knew how damaging to any community it is when there is constant criticism, attacking, fighting. Benedict advocated that peace begin within the individual, by his or her working for personal growth and trying to understand and accept others. "To become positive people who can build up without destroying others: this is one of the most important challenges Benedict sets before us today."[20]

Benedictine peace includes living in Christ and witnessing to a God who created and loves us even though we live in a world that is rife with violence, selfishness, and a type of spiritual bankruptcy. The peace of Benedict's kind rests in God who can bring good out of evil. In her book *Wisdom Distilled from the Daily*, Chittister lists in practical terms what Benedictine spirituality implies for our daily lives and our world as a model of peace.[21] It is worth perusing.

Peace is the result of actually trying to live all the Benedictine values in our little corner of the world. It implies effort, a positive attitude, a deep faith, and daily courage. Peace is a goal to be sought in both our personal and communal worlds. How to attain it is one of Benedict's gifts to the world.

Reflection:

1. Reflect on whether or not you are a positive person. This does not mean ignoring the truth about the bad things that happen or the negative aspect of a bad situation. It does mean that where there is something bad/evil and you are able to address and change it, you are ready to try. In your role as peacemaker you may have to forgive a wrong, find its source and work for truth in the situation. Be courageous enough to confront the issue.

2. Identify ways in which constant criticism is deadly for both the recipient and the "attacker." Can you find ways to counteract it?

3. Pray for peace. Try to unite your will to God's regarding people and events. Act for peace where you perceive injustice and evil.

Humor

"We absolutely condemn in all places any vulgarity and gossip and talk leading to laughter, and we do not permit a disciple to engage in words of that kind" (RB 6.8). "The tenth step of humility is that he [the monk] is not given to ready laughter, for it is written: *Only a fool raises his voice in laughter* (Sir 21:23)" (RB 7.59). "Prefer moderation in speech and speak no foolish chatter, nothing just to provoke laughter; do not love immoderate or boisterous laughter" (RB 4.52-54). After reading these lines from Benedict's Rule, one might wonder how humor can be considered a Benedictine gift and value. Once again, as with humility, one must be careful to relate the text to its time; then, upon reflection, the wisdom will emerge.

First, in order to relate the expressed concepts to our day and present knowledge, it will be relevant to digress a bit and examine what laughter is, or why people laugh. Taking more time to elucidate "humor" may give us some basis for how to relate to Benedict and his time. While this seems like a long, unnecessary digression, it could be foundational to a deeper understanding of the value.

Laughter shows that we have taken pleasure in something. A humorous response involves a complicated mixture of ordinary experience, basic intelligence, social conventions, mental habits, political and religious beliefs, and cultural level. When one perceives an unexpected juxtaposition of two ideas or an unexpected relationship between two judgments, the result is laughter. An example is the limerick or pun that confronts us with two meanings at the same time.

We also laugh because we are capable of introspection, can perceive our own ridiculousness at times, and are capable of guessing what goes on in another's mind. The truly humble person, the self-accepting person, can laugh at himself or herself with great gusto. *True* humor is always in some way a moral affirmation of the dignity of human weakness.

As the world loses its belief in the spiritual, it also loses its area of true humor. For example, it is in the face of a spiritual value that a material value can be ridiculous. The ability to laugh depends on our certitudes because the more certitudes we possess, the more counterfeits of them occur. People who believe in little, laugh little, so the world of the skeptic is utterly humorless. If one considers a chimp to be a sleeping Shakespeare or a Dante, the chimp ceases to be amusing in its behavior. No doubt Benedict had deep spiritual certitudes, but perhaps he did not see their counterfeits as being humorous but rather distracting and even damaging. Remember that in Benedict's time, Western civilization seemed to have disintegrated to the point of decay and disorganization with ceaseless wars, devastated lands, barbaric invasions. Society was corrupt, agriculture and education highly compromised, and many people somewhat demoralized and degenerate.

In reality, humor and religion, hilarity and holiness have something in common. If one knows with certainty where she or he is going, she or he can really enjoy herself or himself better on the way. The real humorist's spirit of playfulness and ability not to take things too seriously comes from a deep intuitive sense that enables her or him to see life in its deeper relationships. Humans laugh because they have a soul (mind, spirit) and since there is a close connection between the spiritual and humor, one of the natural paths to faith and grace may well take us up the pleasant slopes of hilarity. Scripture declares: "For everything there is a season, and a time for every matter under heaven: / a time to be born, and a time to die; / a time to plant, and a time to pluck up what is planted; / a time to kill and a time to heal; / a time to break down, and a time to build; / a time to weep, and a time to laugh" (Eccl 3:1-4).

We now know, from research in our time and in our culture, that laughter is a great workout that boosts the immune system, increases circulation, and offers benefits to the heart. It has positive effects on blood vessels, stress hormones, and mental health. Obviously none of this had been confirmed in Benedict's time.

As Benedict searched the Bible for references to laughter, he would have found relatively few that are positive. (One of the positives would have been Luke 6:21, which reads, "Blessed are you who weep now, for you will laugh.") It seems safe to speculate that the negative references Benedict makes to laughter in his Rule are an effort to prevent any talking that would be derisive of another monk or making fun of a deficiency, deformity, or even idiosyncrasy—laughing at someone or about someone—that would be hurtful to that person or even make him feel less respected, valued, and accepted. Since the monks lived in community, there would have been constant opportunities to observe behavior patterns, character traits, intelligence, naivety, and the like. Opportunities for judging, criticizing, laughing at or about a monk rather than with him would have abounded. We can see from Benedict's efforts to instill respect for others in all who followed his Rule that he did not want snickering or laughter about anyone in his community to interfere with that monk's ability to function as an accepted and appreciated member of the monastic family. Being the frequent butt of jokes or being relegated to the ranks of second-class citizenship does little for self-esteem or peaceful coexistence. No doubt Benedict would have agreed with Johann von Goethe that "by nothing do men show their character more than by the things they laugh at."[22]

A second reason for Benedict's warning about ready laughter may be his effort to keep monks aware of the seriousness of their vocation and search for God. Perhaps he viewed laughter as a type of levity that would distract one from the prime reason for his coming to the monastery and would detract from the transformation the monastic was trying to attain.

Whatever Benedict's reason for his statements about laughter/ humor, it appears safe to conclude that he based his opinion on his studies of previous/early rules and readings, as well as his experiences of life in community. If he were true to form and lived today, he would no doubt incorporate the latest wisdom and knowledge about laughter and humor into his Rule and would be proud of his Benedictine sons, daughters, and oblates who are ready to laugh at themselves and at humorous, unharmful situations. Benedict would probably agree with William Arthur Ward who said: "To make mistakes is human; to stumble is commonplace; to be able to laugh at yourself is maturity."

Going this far afield in our Benedictine-value exposé on humor may be forgiven if we remember with Thomas Merton that "every moment and every event of every man's life on earth plants something in his soul." With that in mind let us beware of taking ourselves too seriously lest we play God.

Reflection

1. At what do you find yourself laughing? What does this say about your self-image?

2. What does Ethel Barrymore mean when she says: "You grow up the day you have your first real laugh at yourself."

3. What is the connection between not taking yourself too seriously and the virtue of humility?

4. How could Reinhold Niebuhr say: "Humour is, in fact, a prelude to faith, and laughter is the beginning of prayer"?

Beauty

It may be futile to try to address beauty because of the different perception each person has of what comprises beauty. Despite that, we are not deterred. Beauty is worthy of discussion not only as a Benedictine value but also as a human need often ignored in our culture. Upon reading the Rule one might wonder how it is possible to extrapolate the idea that beauty is a Benedictine value since there is no direct reference to it. Yet through the centuries, the liturgy, the Scriptoria, the idea that "all utensils and goods of the monastery" are to be regarded "as sacred vessels of the altar" (RB 31.10), the acknowledgment and even promotion of artisans of the monastery (RB 57) point to a type of stewardship and reverence for the beautiful. Whether copying the words of Scripture and adorning them with beautiful illuminations, or interpreting them in visual illustrations, or weaving reverent, haunting chant melodies around the words for liturgical services; whether working in mosaics, painting on glass, carving wood, working in gold, silver, iron, brass; designing vestments and stitching the designs with intricate, colorful needlework, Benedictine monastics have proved their love for beauty. They also preserved the writings of the fathers and classical authors with a calligraphy that is artistic in itself. The penmanship of the copyists can be considered beautiful.

From the earliest times the arts and crafts (as well as sciences) found their home in the Benedictine monastery. Benedict's reference to the artisans of the monastery (RB 57) gives evidence of that fact. The arts and artisans aspect of the Rule will be dealt with in a later chapter, but it is the focus of this section to ponder the concept of beauty and its value for monastics and all humankind. Several quotes from monastics and other authors will help lay the foundation.

Monastic Thomas Merton says: "One of the most important—and most neglected—elements in the beginning of the interior life is the ability to respond to reality, to see the value and the beauty in ordinary things, to come alive to the splendor that is all around us." Joan Chittister, OSB, writes: "Without the artist to show us what we ourselves do not see of the beauty of the world around us, we lose sight of the beauty of God as well. . . . The function of the artist in the monastery—and in the life of us all—is to make the transcendent visible; to touch the soul in ways that match the soul; to enshrine beauty so that we may learn to see it; and to make where we live places of wonder."[23] "Truth, and goodness, and beauty are but different faces of the same all" (Ralph Waldo Emerson). "Love beauty; it is the shadow of God on the universe" (Gabriela Mistral). "Beauty on occasion provides an opportunity for the transcendent to break through briefly into our lives and illumine them."[24] "All artists, in addition to opening us to beauty, teach us truths about our relationship to God, ourselves, and others."[25] "We must seek beauty, study beauty, surround ourselves with beauty. To revivify the soul of the world, we ourselves must become beauty . . . To be contemplative we must remove the clutter from our lives, surround ourselves with beauty, and consciously, relentlessly, persistently, give it away until the tiny world for which we ourselves are responsible begins to reflect the raw beauty that is God."[26]

When we encounter true beauty we can be so overwhelmed that it brings tears to our eyes or stops our breath, or even calls us to some deeper truth or good. We are surrounded by the beauty that God created. It is all around us in such "things" as a red-gold sunset over the shimmering waters of a lake; the unique patterns of each snowflake; the smile of a child. God speaks to us constantly through the beauty that surrounds us. Beautiful things and experiences of beauty are sacraments that bring God closer and touch us with grace. Beauty can throw light on our world of reality and help disclose the truth about ourselves, our world, our being, even our "destiny." Have you ever been lifted beyond the now by some lovely Mozart aria or a Van Gogh painting, or a poem or film that touches your deepest self? Beauty can show God to the world in many ways; it can lead us to truth and incline us to goodness if we are open to its reality. "Beauty is Being breaking through to assure us of Its benignity. . . . Encounters of beauty do open us up to their own alchemy, which gently guides us to goodness and truth."[27] Is it any wonder that Benedictines value beauty and have espoused it from the beginning of their founding?

Benedictine spirituality recognizes with John O'Donohue that "the human soul is hungry for beauty; we seek it everywhere—in landscape, music, art, clothes, furniture, gardening, companionship, love, religion and in ourselves. . . . We feel most alive in the presence of the Beautiful for it meets the needs of our soul."[28]

Reflection

1. Stop and reflect on how the vulgar, ugly, and artificial affect your mind, heart, and even body.

2. What is the difference between glamor and beauty?

3. Do the media attempt to give us beauty or are they more prone to deliver things that are violent and downright ugly?

4. Reflect on our films. Do they aim to uplift or rather to titillate, excite, frighten?

5. What percentage of our computer and video games invite us to positive actions that uplift the mind and heart rather than show negativity and annihilation of something or someone?

Moderation

Moderation is one of the principles that courses through Benedict's Rule. Whether we term it a value, an ideal, or something else, Benedict obviously saw it as a virtue to be sought after and gained. In ordering monastic life Benedict speaks of the amount of food, drink, clothing, and work, and after stating the initial provision, he invariably adds an exception, all still within the realm of moderation. Benedict wanted to avoid the tyranny of extremes for his monks. Here are some examples from the Rule. "Refrain from too much eating or sleeping, and *from laziness* (Rom 12:11)" (RB 4.36-38). "In these [Sunday] Vigils, too, there must be moderation in quantity" (RB 11.2). (Here Benedict is referring to the number of psalms and readings.) "Prefer moderation in speech" (RB 4.52). In chapter 31, verse 12, Benedict requires that the cellarer of the monastery "should not be prone to greed, nor be wasteful and extravagant with the goods of the monastery, but should do everything with moderation and according to the abbot's orders."

In chapter 39, on "The Proper Amount of Food," Benedict suggests that there be two kinds of cooked food, but a third dish of fruit or fresh vegetables might be added plus a generous pound of bread per day. If the monks' work is heavier, the abbot may decide on something additional, but overindulgence must be avoided "lest a monk experience indigestion." Chapter 40 on "The Proper Amount of Drink" begins thus: "*Everyone has his own gift from God, one this and another that* (1 Cor 7:7). It is, therefore, with some uneasiness that we specify the amount of food and drink for others." Then Benedict takes the plunge anyway and goes on to share his opinion about what amount of wine he thinks sufficient. He allows the superior to determine "when local conditions, work or the summer heat indicates the need for a greater amount. He [the superior] must, in any case, take great care lest excess or drunkenness creep in" (RB 40.5). Benedict continues: "We read that monks should not drink wine at all, but since the monks of our day cannot be convinced of this, let us at least agree to drink moderately, and not to the point of excess" (RB 40.6).

When sharing his thoughts about specified times for labor and prayerful reading, Benedict adds: "Yet, all things are to be done with moderation on account of the faint-hearted" (RB 48.9). Benedict also discusses the amount of clothing, footwear, and bedding he considers necessary for his monks. Then, always taking into account the climate and other conditions, he adds: "the Abbot is to provide all things necessary: that is, cowl, tunic, sandals, shoes, belt, knife, stylus, needle, handkerchief and writing tablets" (RB 55.18-19). Benedict advises the abbot to remember that "*distribution was made to each one as he had need* (Acts 4:35)," then reminds the abbot to "take into account the weaknesses of the needy, not the evil will of the envious" (RB 55.20-21). Note that the key word here is *need*, not desire.

One last quote from the Rule should suffice and convince. In chapter 70, verses 4 through 5, Benedict says: "Boys up to the age of fifteen should, however, be carefully controlled and supervised by everyone, provided that this too is done with moderation and common sense."[29]

Note the frequency of exceptions, the concern for cultural and climatic differences, the awareness of different types of human beings, and the variation in their needs. Benedict allows for necessities but eschews extremes. The wise Benedict, steeped in knowledge of Scripture, church fathers, and other writers, having promoted equality in his monastery, would no doubt have agreed with Aristotle that "the virtue of justice consists in moderation, as regulated by wisdom." Aware of each of his monk's constant need for conversion and transformation, Benedict would probably also have agreed with Jean Paul Richter who said: "Only actions give life strength; only moderation gives it charm."

Though the topic of sin is not very popular these days, it might be relevant to address it here. Whether one considers sin a transgression against moral law or merely terms it a type of offense or violation, it will, in the long run, not make life really happy or fulfilling. For our purposes here, we will touch on sin only as a means to better understand the value of moderation. What are commonly known as the seven capital sins are, in reality, extremes, excesses. If we think about it, pride is but a form of inordinate self-love/self-esteem; greed, an immoderate love for riches; lust, an excessive indulgence in sexual pleasure; gluttony, the overindulgence in food or drink; and so on. On the other hand their opposites may also be far from virtuous. Having too little self-esteem does not praise our generous, loving Creator; eating too little can damage the body, lead to anorexia, compromise our health. You can ponder the rest. It appears that to do things in moderation; to control ourselves, is to move down a type of middle path that leads to virtue. Perhaps that is why Joseph Hall said: "Moderation is the silken string running through the pearl chain of all virtues."

Can one also take virtues to extremes that are not healthy? Is being too brave foolhardy, while not being brave enough, cowardly? Can an employer be so patient with an ineffective employee that she or he is enabling the ineffectiveness? Or can the employer be so impatient that her or his anger paralyzes the employee's efforts and impedes personal, spiritual growth? What about the virtue of love? Can parental love of a child be considered a virtue if that love does not help the child grow in self-discipline, self-control, respect for others? Should it not be called neglect or fear of rejection, and will that child not grow into a grasping, selfish, unhappy adult? Similarly, is love *really* love when there is excessive control, constant nagging, even severe physical punishment? Is that not really a form of abuse rather than love? Once again we are confronted with the truth that even virtues seem to benefit from moderation.

Aristotle advises: "It is better to rise from life as from a banquet—neither thirsty nor drunken." We agree with Casey who suggests that moderation is not easy to observe. What *is* too much or too little? We might think we should let common sense prevail. For some that may be helpful, but is common sense really common? Wisdom, on the other hand, is a type of baptized common sense infused with consistent efforts to listen to an all-loving God, and applying that to lived experience. Benedict had a lifetime of that type of effort and application. Why not be like Benedict and let wisdom lead the way because moderation is a key virtue from which, as Goethe says, "pure happiness springs."

Reflection

1. What does Pascal mean when he says: "To go beyond the bounds of moderation is to outrage humanity"?

2. Have you personally experienced the effects of excessive drinking, eating? What were the damaging results physically, psychologically, emotionally?

3. Is self-discipline necessary for emotional maturity? Give reasons for your answer.

4. What is the relationship between moderation and self-control?

Compassion

Thomas Aquinas said that he would rather feel compassion than know the meaning of it. Wouldn't we all! Despite that, since knowledge may lead to action, we shall set up our quotes from Benedict's Rule by first referring to some thoughts about compassion from other sources.

The dictionary defines compassion as "the deep feeling of sharing the suffering of another, together with the inclination to give aid or support or to show mercy." Daniel Goleman states: "The act of compassion begins with our full attention. . . . You have to really see the person. . . . Self-absorption in all its forms kills empathy, let alone compassion. . . . When we focus on others our world expands." Henry Ward Beecher was convinced that "compassion will cure more sins than condemnation." Albert Schweitzer wrote: "Until he extends his circle of compassion to all living things, man will not himself find peace." Thomas Merton said: "The whole idea of compassion is based on a keen awareness of the interdependence of all these living beings, which are all part of one another, and all involved in one another."

As we move through Benedict's Rule we will find much evidence that, as he wrote it, he must have pondered both the individual human being and human beings in their relationships. Throughout his Rule, Benedict conveys an awareness of both individual needs and communal good, once again displaying his knowledge of human nature. As you read these passages remember that they were written in the sixth century, a time when the social and cultural life was deteriorating and depravity was prevalent. The Prologue states, "Therefore we intend to establish a school for the Lord's service. In drawing up its regulations we hope to set down nothing harsh, nothing burdensome" (45-46). Can you already see a certain compassion peeking through these words?

Remember that with the collapse of the Roman Empire in the fifth century, a type of social chaos prevailed. Life was often not safe. There was a breakdown of law and order because there was little to take the place of the collapsed government structure. The Romans had had relatively efficient agriculture, extensive road networks, water-supply systems, and shipping routes that began to decay. Barbarians raided and killed residents of villages across Europe and those surviving could not grow food. The decay of what had been a type of social cohesion also affected the cultural unity and artistic and scholarly endeavors. Benedictine monasticism was a wonderful gift in the midst of this chaos, providing a sense of stability and peace for those who had experienced or were experiencing war, invasion, vandalism, brutality, and internal and external instability and chaos. Whether some of these people came to the monastery as guests or potential monks, Benedict would treat them with compassion. These excerpts from the Rule will show that Benedict was in tune with the social and cultural conditions of the times when he gave his advice about how to treat these human beings, how to receive and care for them.

"Never give a hollow greeting of peace or turn away when someone needs your love" (RB 4.25). A monk who has transgressed "should be warned twice privately by the seniors" before being rebuked publicly (RB 23.1-3). At first glance this may not seem like a type of compassion, but recall the breakdown of society, and this does show sensitivity to one who may be extremely undisciplined. While Benedict is not speaking of the type of warning we may receive while speeding, could we use this as a limping analogy and reminder that in our day, after the initial warning to the offending driver, if there is a further speeding offense there is a "public" fine to be paid and public notice in the newspaper (or at least on the driver's record).

"The abbot must exercise the utmost care and concern for wayward brothers, because *it is not the healthy who need a physician, but the sick* (Matt. 9:12)" (RB 27.1). Benedict asks the abbot to send mature, wise brothers who secretly support and console the wayward one. He asks that they should reaffirm him (the offender) in love and pray for him. "He [the abbot] should realize that he has undertaken care of the sick, not tyranny over the healthy" (RB 27.6). "He [the abbot] is to imitate the loving example of the Good Shepherd who left the ninety-nine sheep in the mountains and went in search of the one sheep that had strayed. So great was his compassion for its weakness that *he* mercifully *placed it on his* sacred *shoulders* and so carried it back to the flock (Luke 15:5)" (RB 27.8-9).

In Benedict's monastery the cellarer was in charge of the material things. The Rule not only reminds the *abbot* to be compassionate in his dealings but also reminds the *cellarer* of his duties in that regard. If the cellarer has to deny an unreasonable demand he should "reasonably and humbly deny the improper request" (RB 31.7). In chapter 31, verse 9, Benedict says, "He [the cellarer] must show every care and concern for the sick, children, guests and the poor." Benedict is consistent in his awareness of the truly needy and marginalized. In our own time and culture we frequently hear of child abuse, neglect of health care for the needy, and increasing levels of poverty often fueled by the greed of corporations and conscienceless individuals. The Rule reminds us to live the corporal and spiritual works of mercy. In his chapter on "The Tools for Good Works," Benedict says: "Go to help the troubled and console the sorrowing" (RB 4.18). This chapter is full of scriptural quotes and spiritual "tasks" that, when lived daily, will yield the type of spiritual growth that leads to eternal joy with God.

Continuing effort to mine more nuggets of compassion in the Rule leads us to chapter 36, verses 1 through 3: "Care of the sick must rank above and before all else, so that they may be truly served as Christ." "Although human nature itself is inclined to be compassionate toward the old and the young, the authority of the rule should also provide for them. Since their lack of strength must always be taken into account, they should certainly not be required to follow the strictness of the rule with regard to food, but should be treated with kindly consideration and allowed to eat before the regular hours" (RB 37.1-2). "Brothers who are sick or weak should be given a type of work or craft that will keep them busy without overwhelming them or driving them away. The abbot must take their infirmities into account" (RB 48.24-25). Benedict even discusses the kitchen servers, reminding his monks that "the brothers should serve one another" but those who are not strong must have help "so that they may serve without distress" (RB 35.1, 3).

Regarding clothing and footwear the abbot is reminded that he must consider the weaknesses of the needy (see RB 55). The abbot receives further reminders in chapter 64. He "must hate faults but love the brothers" (11). When pruning faults he must use prudence and love according to what he sees is best for each individual and avoid extremes. He should be discerning and moderate in assigning tasks and "arrange everything that the strong have something to yearn for and the weak nothing to run from" (RB 64.19). The abbot must be "chaste, temperate and merciful. He should always *let mercy triumph over judgment* (Jas 3:13)" (RB 64.9-10).

Our final citation concerning compassion in the Rule says something about Benedict's hopes for and experience during Liturgy of the Hours. It might bring a smile. He shows compassion for his monks and all his guests when he says: "No one should presume to read or sing unless he is able to benefit the hearers" (RB 47.3). Since the central part of Benedictine monastic life is the "Work of God" (*Opus Dei*), otherwise known as Liturgy of the Hours, it would have been, in Benedict's time and still today, extremely painful and even draining to try to attend to the Work of God when there is frequent distraction because of flatness or dissonance in pitch, variation in tempo, a grating timbre in the singing, a lack of comprehension of the text, or no vocal projection from the reader. Ask any monastic who encounters such things day by day and you will receive gratitude for Benedict's gentle reminder about the reader and singer.

Lest we get lost in the many passages quoted above, we can tie them all together in a type of summation. For Benedict, the abbot is to be a loving father, an instrument of God's divine kindness and goodness. The scripturally minded Benedict does not hesitate to ask his superiors to remember their own frailty when dealing with offenders; to recall that they themselves are not without faults. The abbot and those in authority are to know their monks as individuals, beloved of God. The abbot should strive to attain this ideal because he has in his community a variety of temperaments: persons with varying intelligence, needs, abilities, character strengths, and weaknesses. When he knows them, he can adapt to each, be flexible, deal with them with wisdom and love. The sick, the weak, the sinful are recognized as such and are dealt with accordingly as by a wise physician, a good shepherd, a loving father.

Guests and visitors to the monastery are to be received as Christ. Benedict's insistence on this is taken seriously by contemporary monastics, however busy their lives are. Welcoming a constant stream of guests at all hours of the day calls for a certain patience, self-discipline, and a kindness that emanates from the Christ within the monastic whose quiet time, duties, and plans may have been frequently interrupted.

The cellarer in our day is one who oversees the material aspects of the monastery and dispenses its goods. In Saint Benedict's Monastery in Saint Joseph, Minnesota, the duties of the cellarer may be said to be divided between the treasurer or financial director, the physical plant manager, and those bearing various subtitles who support them. This group sees to the daily needs of the monastic community. In accord with the desire of Benedict they are to be compassionate, patient, humble, and kind. The Rule is countercultural insofar as it charges the person in authority not to exert power over the needy as though she or he is doing them a favor by supplying what is needed. Rather, those in need are to be treated with love and mercy. How does this type of attitude and approach play out in twenty-first-century America?

Benedict was keenly aware that God showed his compassion to humanity by sending us Christ. Christ—the manifestation of love, concern, compassion. How often does Scripture detail Christ's being moved to heal the sick, to forgive, to accept, and to associate with those whom society and church leaders considered unacceptable? How the "rejects" of that time must have reached out with hope to this loving human being! The presence of Christ in our midst gave us humans a model of compassion personified. Benedict strives for that same Christ-like presence in the midst of and throughout his community. He asks it of his community leaders and of his monks in their relationship to strangers and each other. When discussing the Rule of Benedict, compassion is a quality/value not mentioned as frequently as others. It deserves to be a key focus of all who aim to live Benedictine spirituality.

Reflection

1. Identify an act of compassion toward you that has had a profound effect on your spiritual, social, physical, material/financial life.

2. What is the social climate, the attitude, of twenty-first-century America toward its needy, weak, sick, and sinful?

3. Name a person in your personal life, or in the national or international realm, whom you consider to be compassionate. What have they done to earn that label?

4. How can you as a parent apply Benedict's idea of compassion to your children?

5. How can you as a teacher apply Benedict's idea of loving kindness to your students?

6. Is there relevance for you as a CEO or business owner in Benedict's expectations of how to treat his monks?

7. Identify areas in your personal social/cultural life where you could be more compassionate.

8. What spiritual steps do you personally have to take to allow God's loving kindness to flow through you to others?

Important Elements of Benedictine Life

Lectio Divina

Saint Benedict considered *lectio* so vital to his spirituality and the monastic life that he wrote it into his Rule as something to be practiced several hours daily. Through *lectio* we can meet God in his word if we are present to God and deeply listening. In *lectio*

God can speak to us directly, one-to-one, as a friend, as one who loves us. The text can serve "as a mirror that brings inner realities to consciousness. . . . In *lectio* the intention is affective not cognitive, it is a work of a heart that desires to make contact with God and, thereby, to reform our lives."[30]

As we practice *lectio* daily, the Word, the living presence of God, can give us personal insights that can lead us to conversion of life, to a healthy, holistic living, and to a keen sensitivity to what God is calling us to be and asking us to do for those whom we meet and for the world. Thus *lectio divina*, the prayerful reading of Scripture, spiritual writings, mystics, and contemporary prophets, invites us to listen and respond so that we can be transformed. If we are faithful to *lectio*, we will eventually put on Christ, find God's presence in the ordinary things of life, and grow in self-knowledge and inner peace.

How should oblates of Saint Benedict practice *lectio divina* (holy reading)? You may use the following procedure and you will find additional outlines in appendix C. Some will be similar but not exactly the same.

Choose a text from Scripture or sacred reading, or choose a life experience. Create for yourself an environment conducive to prayer and quiet and choose a time of about twenty minutes in length (preferably the same time every day) to devote to *lectio* but reserve an alternate time if necessary. Make sure to choose a quiet place. Hopefully it is not a work place but if there is no other alternative, clear away whatever might be a distraction. Sit comfortably. When these physical externals have been taken care of, close your eyes to quiet your mind and body, sitting very still for a few minutes as you ask the Holy Spirit to guide you. Then begin.

1. *Lectio*: Read the Sacred Scripture text (or whatever sacred text is chosen) slowly. Reading it out loud can be helpful. Read the text a second time, even a third if you choose, and stop at a word or phrase that touches you. (Write it in your journal if you choose.)

2. *Meditatio*: Why does this word or phrase touch you? Repeat the word/phrase, reflect on it. What memories or life connections does it invoke? What are your feelings? Do not be afraid

of your feelings or judge them as good or bad. Don't even judge your thoughts (e.g., "I shouldn't think this"). (Write in your journal if you choose.)

3. *Oratio*: Prayer. Response of the heart to God. Speak to God about your experience. Listen to what God says to you. To what are you being called? How/where are you being invited to change? Be aware of God's presence. (Write in your journal if you choose.)

4. *Contemplatio*: Contemplation. Just be present to the God who is eternally present in you. Rest in your (above) reflection, insight, prayer, feeling. "Be still and know that I am God." Rest in God's embrace.

5. *Compassio*: Compassion. This is one of the fruits of prayer and contemplation "in which our whole being is opened up to experience the brokenness of all creation" and "we find ourselves united to God and to all who live."

6. *Operatio*: Action. God calls, invites us to act to help others, and empowers us to do so.

There are many fine publications on *lectio divina*. You have only to access them in bookstores, libraries, and online. You will find some listed in the bibliography of this book. The more frequently you do *lectio*, the more comfortable you will feel with it. You will find your own style. Please do not consider yourself locked into a formula for prayer. Use *lectio* as a way to connect with God on a deep personal level.

While Scripture is an ideal source for *lectio*, there are spiritual writers throughout the centuries who offer profound texts, insights, and opportunities for personal spiritual growth and for helping to weave God through your life. Feel free to use them. You can also use icons, other works of art, a life event, poetry, or a hymn/text as a type of sacred reading that can have God speaking to you.

Liturgy: Office of the Hours

Benedict asks that "nothing is to be preferred to the Work of God" (RB 43.3). He considers prayer so important that he wrote chapters 8 through 20 on it. In chapter 19, verses 1 to 2, he says: "We believe that the divine presence is everywhere and *that in every place the eyes of the Lord are watching the good and the wicked* (Prov 15:3). But beyond the least doubt we should believe this to be especially true when we celebrate the divine office." No wonder he takes such pains to make sure that periods of community prayer are woven throughout each day. In this way, Benedict not only keeps bringing us back to God's presence in our daily life but also, in some sense, helps us to keep life in perspective and sanctify the time of our days. Since the Benedictine truly seeks God, these communal and personal encounters with God throughout the day serve as a refocusing of why we are here, in this monastery, in this world. But knowing human nature, Benedict asks us to make a special effort to see that "our minds are in harmony with our voices" (RB 19.7).

Oblates pray some part of the Divine Office wherever they are located and they are assured of the spiritual connection to their monastery through the prayer of the monastics. Saint Benedict's Monastery, for example, prays the Divine Office daily at Morning Prayer, Noon Prayer, and Evening Prayer. On Saturday nights there is also Vigil. The psalms are the core of the Divine Office along with Scripture readings and canticles. While the thought of repeating 150 psalms over and over may telegraph boredom to the uninitiated, one finds that the psalms not only recount salvation history but also express many aspects of our emotional lives, even the call to God out of the darkness of despair. As we pray them the psalms can become the voice of God revealing ourselves and our world to us and expanding our hearts as we offer God praise, gratitude, and trust in God's promises. We may even start to acquire an inner peace as we begin to absorb the fact of God's goodness and unconditional love toward humans throughout history and in the present.

Wise Benedict looked at the seasons, looked at the hours of our days, and marked them out in such a way as to sanctify time and hopefully sanctify us along with it, as we return the gift of time to God consistently and at periods woven throughout the day. Oblates are always invited to join monastics in praying the Divine Office and in attending the daily Eucharistic celebration. There are also breviaries available for home use, and some prayers of this type can be found online. Examples of Morning Prayer, Evening Prayer, and Compline are given in appendix B of this book.

Eucharist

Obviously the Eucharist is the ultimate prayer in which Jesus continues to offer himself for all people in order to heal and sanctify the world. At the Eucharist we can offer ourselves with Christ and pray for our own needs and the needs of others and all creation. At the Eucharist we can again focus on the meaning and gift of Christ as we let go of our daily cares and place them in God's loving hands. As we experience God's presence in the Word and in the spiritually nourishing body and blood of Christ, we have centered our thoughts, for that span of time, and given our presence to the mystery of our salvation and our "god-ness" through Christ. When we give God the gift of time by attending the Eucharist we have placed ourselves in a position to encounter God's presence in a concrete way. We can then move out into our daily activities and relationships as a more keenly aware instrument of God for others.

The consciousness of our God-union can intensify even more through *daily* attendance at Eucharist where we live the Christ-centered liturgical year with the church and its saints (who offer further examples of full Christian living). The graces we receive through the Eucharist can renew and strengthen us for our daily challenges, tasks, and service. When we gather in spiritual community as the Mystical Body of Christ at Eucharist, we open ourselves to experience the mystery of what it means to be the people of God. In the Word, Christ speaks to us, and we will hear what is frequently so relevant to our lives. Then, with an attitude of reverence, trust, self-surrender, we receive the God who made us, loves us, wills our good, and will never leave us.

Oblates treasure the Eucharist and enter into it with the full participation that leads to fathoming the mystery and reaping the graces that aid their daily lives with all its joys, sorrows, and challenges. All are always welcome to attend Eucharist at Benedictine monasteries.

Societal and Social Justice Concerns

Saint Benedict asks that we serve one another; that we listen to each other; that we become aware. We are also to be careful not to call anything our own (RB 33.1-3, 6), meaning we should not be attached to things. Our culture, on the other hand, urges us to keep on acquiring, to get the latest gadget, the "new and improved" product, until our homes are bulging with even unnecessary things and three or four garages house our many adult "toys."

Benedict wants us to always act out of love, to be hospitable, to be Christ *for* others and *to* others. We are to show respect, patience, forbearance; we are to care, to have compassion. Guests are to be treated as Christ regardless of who they are.

These few references to Benedict's expectations (there are many more that are applicable) all imply that we must reach out of ourselves toward our neighbor regardless of his or her creed or color. We must use our knowledge and our gifts to help the poor, the lonely, the forgotten. We must manage our resources wisely and use the gift of God's good earth not as owners but as stewards. Benedict urges reverence for all creation. That includes soil, water, the air we breathe, the trees we plant, the plants we tend, the pets we adopt. It includes, above all, reverence for human life whether in embryo or old age. It includes reverence of the sick, the dying, the helpless, the impaired, the voiceless, the insignificant, remembering to accord them the dignity they deserve.

If everything in our life is God's gift and sacred, what happens when we look around and see pollution, greed, arrogance, waste, destruction of our environment? What happens to the "common good" when the lust for power and control, and the need for more and more profits dominate individual, business, and governmental actions? When violence is used to attain personal ends, and we live in such a way as to think only of ourselves and our pleasures, what will happen to how we treat others and the earth? When we are gentle with ourselves and one another, when we respect others, are kind to them and think of their needs, when we try to be open to each other and work for peace and community building, when we treasure our gifts of earth and all life, then we are carrying on the Benedictine tradition and are really trying to live Benedictine spirituality.

Stewardship and Care for the Environment

Benedict wants us to treat things as if they were "vessels of the altar" (RB 31.10). In chapter 32, Saint Benedict says: "Whoever fails to keep the things belonging to the monastery clean or treats them carelessly should be reproved" (4). He wants us to be aware of the sacredness of things and take responsibility for what God has given us; to take care of what we have. In chapter 33 he reminds us that we do not have private ownership of things but hold them in common. In chapter 34, Benedict provides that distribution of goods be made according to need.

In the section titled "Of All Good Gifts," in the document *Upon This Tradition* (1980), the American Benedictine Sisters articulated some thoughts for living out Benedict's view of stewardship in our time. They assert: "In ways never before faced in history, we realize that the planet is unitary, the population interdependent, and the possibility of human destruction real. Someone must steward the world" (76). They continue: "In light of the incarnation, we recognize the holiness of earth, the oneness of humanity, and the transcendence of selfless love over selfishness in every form" (78).

Benedict was in tune with nature, and with the rhythm of the days and seasons. His reverence for all things includes the land and the environment. The fact that we are responsible for the good of all people and all created things is certainly antithetical to a culture that frequently wastes resources and pollutes both air and water. Stewardship for Benedictines means that we must continue to work toward keeping the earth and our environment wholesome and healthy and join with those who have made a start to do so. We try to use the goods of the earth wisely, remembering that God created all things to be in balance and harmony, not abused or wasted. Modern war and industrial greed are among the chief threats to life on this planet. If we are manipulated by the bureaucracy and forget that all inhabitants of the globe are one, will there ever be the peace we so desire? If we are like Benedict we will work for peace and the common good in our own communities, in our own little corner of the world.

Equality and Uniqueness of Persons

As we read the Rule of Benedict we find that, sprinkled through-out its pages, is the message that we are all equal and we are not to judge others or decide their value based on social clan, wealth, or position. Benedict exhorts us to listen to, respect, reverence, accept all, and love all people, treating each one as we would Christ. The message that we must accept people as they are and recognize them as unique individuals comes through loud and clear. In chapter 2, "The Qualities of the Abbot," we read that the abbot should avoid all favoritism and show equal love to everyone. Benedict reminds the abbot that he must vary his approach according to the circumstances. "With the undisciplined and restless, he will use firm argument; with the obedient and docile and patient, he will appeal for greater virtue" (RB 2.25). The abbot is advised to remember that he is serving a variety of temperaments and "must accommodate and adapt himself to each one's character and intelligence" (RB 2.32). In chapter 64 the abbot is reminded that when dealing with faults he should work in a way that seems best for each individual and should "so arrange everything that the strong have something to yearn for and the weak nothing to run from" (RB 64.19).

Distribution of goods is to be made according to need (RB 34). Care of the sick, elderly, and children is noted (RB 36–37). Individual needs are also considered when Benedict discusses food and clothing (RB 39, 55). In determining monastic rank Benedict says that the date of entry into the monastery is the key factor "regardless of age or distinction" (RB 63.8). Guests, regardless of who they are, are to be received as Christ.

Benedict is steeped in the Scriptures and has thoroughly imbibed the good news of Christ that proclaimed the value of each human being and the truth that "*whether slave or free, we are all one in Christ* (Gal 3:28; Eph 6:8)" (RB 2.20).

When oblates live out Benedictine spirituality in their ordinary, daily lives, they are truly living as Christ and with Christ. When this is done in a self-seeking society it is obviously countercultural. Oblates know that if they should suffer in their efforts to counteract prejudices, arrogance, violence, poverty, and whatever evil they encounter, their monastic community is here to support them in whatever way possible.

Sacredness of Life

To reiterate what has been previously stressed: Benedict urged the monks to "regard all utensils and goods of the monastery as sacred vessels of the altar" (RB 31.10). If he felt that way about material things there can be no doubt about what he felt regarding nature, human beings, all of creation. "Sacred" is the applicable word to all God created. To see with the heart of Christ, as Benedictines are committed to do, means that we know we are all God's people, made in God's image, and that our God is love. As monastics and oblates we must nurture, live, and share this conviction in the midst of a "throwaway" society. In seeking to be aware of our God, ourselves, our neighbor, and the sacredness of all creation, and acting accordingly, we will continue to encounter opposition and even ridicule from those who espouse a materialistic, hedonistic philosophy. When we promote the oneness of all creation we are immediately embracing not only the concept of the Creator but also the concept of creation, *in all its forms*. We respect and accrue dignity to the physically and mentally challenged, the poor, the unborn, the elderly, the stranger, the abused, the persecuted, the hungry, the power-less, the disenfranchised. The list goes on and on as the implications of our assertions open out into the realm of daily life and actions.

As Benedictines, we want to build community within the monastery and the world. At the basis of this is respect for each person and the belief that every human being is sacred and has a right to develop his or her talents, gifts, potential. When materialism, profit, and power dominate the political and economic systems, there is little thought given to the needy individual and the common good. How can we witness to the sacredness of life? Some of the ways are: educating, taking social action by joining groups that feed and clothe the needy, paying a just wage, helping the jobless find employment, visiting the sick and elderly and those in nursing homes, using material things and gifts of nature reverently, not wasting, and being aware of being manipulated by consumerism. All creatures are precious in the sight of their Creator. As Benedictine oblates we recognize this and live accordingly.

Leisure

Benedictine spirituality is one of balance. There is work, prayer, reading, and time for reflection. The implication in Benedict's making time for reading and thoughtful "pondering" is that all human beings have a need for restful and reenergizing periods if they are to stay wholesome, healthy, balanced. Periods of rest and reflection can take us out of our hectic, fast-paced, product-producing activities and help us to realize the meaning of life as we think about not only doing but also *being*. Benedict's leisure aims at enhancing our understanding of life, of who we are, of who we are meant to be in the eyes of God. It allows us (and asks us) to step off the treadmill of daily doing and delve into the meaning of things, to try to see how God is at work in our lives, in our world. When we live a life that is aware of the God in us, in others, in the world around us, when we are no longer focused totally on our own little world and personal agenda, we have stopped living superficially and have started to become anchored in deeper realities. In other words, we have started to become contemplatives. "The genius of Benedictinism is its concentration on living the active life contemplatively."[31]

The kind of leisure Benedict advocates is that which leads to enhancing our understanding of life's meaning and recharges the soul. It slows us down, takes us aside and, with effort on our part, removes us from our overstimulated environments for some time each day so that we can try to connect with the God within us and within all things.

Benedictine leisure is sometimes termed "holy leisure" or "sacred leisure." It embraces the qualities of silence, openness, and presence to the now and to the Creator. It is not selfish; rather, it can make us more human and deepen our understanding of what is important in life. It nourishes the mind and soul as it helps us encounter the living God and helps fill the emptiness in the inner core of ourselves.

Throughout the centuries, as monastics have adapted to the needs of the person and to humankind in our changing and evolving culture, they have also recognized the "play" aspect of leisure as a means of relaxation, of refreshing body and mind. A quick walk through the beauties of nature can jump start reflection on, and conversation with, God. Hobbies can bring out creative talents not otherwise used. Games and sports can provide physical exercise and also reduce stress. Some good literature and audiovisual entertainment (concerts, plays, movies, television shows) can help us escape the pressures of everyday life and connect us with our fellow humans. Yet, though all of these leisure activities (and the many not mentioned here) are basically good, healthful, and refreshing, they should never replace or substitute for that "holy leisure" that Benedictine spirituality treasures and promotes, because it is that "sacred reading" time during which we more directly and consciously seek for and encounter the living God.

The Arts and Artisans / Beauty

Benedict wants the artists of the monastery to use their gifts in all humility and, basically, to recognize those gifts as a type of participation in God's beauty and creation. Throughout their monastic history, Benedictines have accepted artists into their communities, have fostered their gifts, and have, in general, patronized the arts. The history of Western civilization is replete with examples of the contribution of Benedictines to the arts. One need only look at the illuminated manuscripts of the Gospels and other works produced or copied in the monastic Scriptorium to realize the value that the Benedictines placed on books and education. The monks and nuns copied not only Scripture but also the church fathers, the classical literature of Greece and Rome, and the stories of their ancestral people. We will address this love for books later. What of the other arts?

In the realm of Benedictine architecture, one has only to look at the great abbeys of Europe and their churches to begin to realize the artistic and cultural activities that took place there. Monte Cassino, Canterbury, York, Cluny; frescoes, paintings, metal work, stained glass, sculpture—all attest to the artists and artistic endeavors themselves or to the attainment and support of them by Benedictines through the centuries. These buildings, these Benedictine monasteries, became centers for civilizing their surroundings and also sources of Western Christian culture.

The art of music owes much to the Benedictines who first notated the plain chant (Gregorian chant), helped establish music theory, worked with developing vocal polyphony, and by the tenth century were using the pipe organ as instrumental accompaniment in their abbey churches. The chant repertory included music for

Mass, the Liturgy of the Hours, and the liturgical year itself. The Benedictine monk, Guido d' Arezzo (AD 995–1050) developed the four-line staff for the notation of chant. This became the standard staff used for Gregorian chant and might be considered the forerunner of our present five-line staff. Gregorian chant has been preserved by Benedictines throughout the centuries. The abbey church of Cluny, considered to be one of the marvels of the Middle Ages, resounded with Gregorian chant, which was an essential part of its many liturgies and rituals. Cluny was a center of scholarship, the arts, music, and cultural activity from the beginning of the tenth century to the middle of the twelfth.

In the nineteenth century the Abbey of Solesmes helped to restore the earlier and more pure state of the chant. After Vatican II, Sister Cecile Gertken, OSB (d. 2001), of Saint Benedict's Monastery, Saint Joseph, Minnesota, fit the ancient chant melodies to the English translations of the new Mass texts. She also translated hymns and antiphons into English and adapted them for the Divine Office. Sister Cecile felt strongly that Gregorian chant needed to be preserved since it could help center the mind and heart on God.

As further bequests by Benedictines to the art of music we cite medieval Benedictine music theorists such as Hucbald and Hermannus Contractus who worked out fundamental concepts regarding the modal system, thus contributing to the element of music tonality.

The solmization system (do-re-mi) developed by the Benedictine Guido d' Arezzo is still used today as a teaching and sight-reading tool. One has only to recall the song "Do, Re, Mi" and how it is used in the musical *The Sound of Music* to see an example of its use and value.

A final example of a Benedictine's personal artistic legacy is that of Abbess Hildegard of Bingen (1098–1179), who, for the last twenty-five years or so, has received international attention and acclaim. She was not only a composer of chants of "stunning originality" but also an artist, a poet, a mystic, and an adviser to popes.

Love of books led monastics to be copyists and binders of books (both metal and leather). In due time, monasteries had their own printing presses. As technology developed, the Benedictines adapted to the times, and they are engaged today even in such areas as designing web pages.

When Benedictines came to America they continued to share their artistic gifts. An example in point is Saint Benedict's Monastery in Saint Joseph, Minnesota, founded in 1857, which has had teachers of music and art as well as musicians, artists, and artisans from its inception to the present. As late as the 1950s there were sisters designing cards and printing them on the monastery press. There were sisters designing and creating vestments, making habits, creating and teaching needlework of all types. There were also candle makers, bookbinders, poets, composers, and craftspeople of all varieties—and this heritage continues. A present-day list of Benedictine artists and artisans at this monastery includes musicians, composers, poets, authors, photographers, to which we can add a weaver, sculptress, and potter as well as card makers, crocheters, doll makers, needleworkers of many forms, and graphic designers. As the list goes on it can expand into cuisine and include outstanding bakers and chefs, winemakers, and, moving outdoors, avid and successful gardeners.

In conclusion we quote: "The particular kind of beauty seen in monastic art is active and dynamic and yet always contains an element of interior silence and peace of heart. The work itself is seen as a continuation of the creative activity of God, bestowing on whatever the form may be—music, architecture, painting, sculpture, handwork—supplemental beauty."[32]

The history of Western civilization is replete with the Benedictine contribution to civilization, education, and the arts. While it is dangerous to generalize, it can be observed that the Benedictines love beauty and have fostered it in varying degrees from their inception to the present. They seek it, promote it, create it. It is their gift from God, to God.

Service

"Therefore we intend to establish a school for the Lord's service" (RB Prol. 45). With these words Benedict sets us on a path that is all-inclusive and all-encompassing. It implies imitation of Christ who always did the will of His Father, gave His life in service to others, and is the model for the Benedictine's and the oblate's self-giving.

To serve in the best sense of the word is to give, assist, aid, nurture, cherish, minister, promote. To serve is to care about and to love. In the monastery (Benedict's school of the Lord's service), the Benedictine monastic learns to live God's basic commandments: to love God above all things and to love one's neighbor as oneself (see Matt 22:37-39). Serving is crucial to the Benedictine life because in serving one learns to reach out, turn from egoism, and open up to relationship with another. For Benedict, to serve the Lord means to serve the *whole* Christ, that is, in effect, the Mystical Body, the church, all the people of God, the world. Service, in Benedictine terms implies and requires (1) prayer and personal self-discipline, which leads to personal transformation and then, by extension, (2) self-forgetfulness, which leads to service of others. In the monastery one serves through such things as presence at liturgy, mutual obedience, attending the sick, sharing in labor, caring for guests, respecting one another, adapting to each temperament, mutual understanding and trust, concern for all in need.

What does it mean to love God with our whole heart and soul? "The love of God translated into human idiom is not just human love that has been somehow blest. Rather, *it is a divine loving that transforms and energizes human loving, so that it is able to do what it could never do alone.*"[33] Could you ever really love or serve your enemy on your own? On your own, could you ever really forgive someone who had killed a loved one or done irreparable harm to those you love? In effect, as God is served, and the Benedictine monastic grows less selfish, becomes more in tune with God's will in the daily, and moves into a deepening relationship with the indwelling Christ, she or he has opened up to becoming an instrument for God's love to be given to others. It will be similar for the oblate who walks the path of Benedictine spirituality.

Benedict lived the Gospel truths and expected his followers to do the same. He wanted to create a community in which each person was treated as an individual with unique gifts and personality. He expected each member to recognize and attend to her or his own physical and spiritual needs and gifts but insisted above all that each one respect the needs of others. He knew and hoped that the love developed through a deep personal relationship with God would then show itself in patience, humility, trust, forgiveness, and kindness. Benedict wanted us to love with the love of Christ. "*They should each try to be the first to show respect to the other* (Rom 12:10), supporting with the greatest patience one another's weaknesses of body or behavior, and earnestly competing in obedience to one another" (RB 72.4-6) "No one is to pursue what he judges better for himself, but instead, what he judges better for someone else" (RB 72.7). How antithetical to the prevailing "me-ism" in our culture! This attitude of self-forgetfulness, of mindfulness of others, does not mean denigration of self but is indicative of, and promotes, the kind of living in Christ's love that then becomes loving as Christ himself loved. By preferring nothing to Christ one can eventually become *as* Christ and can love even one's enemies. Having lived with Christ at the deepest core of their being, Benedictines and oblates can become the concrete reality of both the love of God in them and the love that then most naturally (even urgently and unfailingly) reaches out to the needy, the marginalized, the unloved and unlovable in society. Having known with a certainty the meaning of real love, Benedictine monastics and their oblates can begin to realize in their daily living these words of Christ: "*What you did for one of these least brothers you did for me* (Matt 25:40)" (RB 36.1-3).

While Benedictine monastics are striving to be Christ for each other in their monasteries or wherever their ministries lead them, Benedictine oblates are witnesses of Christ in their own geographical settings, workplaces, and various communities. They can penetrate all areas of life with their Christian example and can reach into every nook and cranny that their lives touch, bringing the Benedictine ideals and values to a hungry, often spiritually blind and bereft world. As men and women of prayer, as faithful readers of Scripture, oblates listen attentively to the spoken Word both in personal Scripture reading and at Eucharist, to discern what God is asking/ telling them. They listen also for God's presence in their daily life experiences and translate what they hear into self-transformation and loving service. As oblates grow ever closer to the God they seek and who seeks them, they become more Christlike, and will increase their service to God and others. Through their personal ongoing efforts at spiritual growth and through their ongoing formation in retreats, days of recollection and renewal, oblates can become consistently more aware of God's presence in the ordinariness of their daily lives and tasks and in those persons whom they meet and with whom they live, work, and worship. They can start to live *as* Christ who did not come to be served but to serve.

For the oblate, being *open* to God and others will lead to mindfulness of God and each human being encountered; it will mean *attending* to God, to God's work and to each other. I ask the reader: As you look at life around you what do you see that needs fixing? Is it the breakdown of marriage and family life; growing greed, materialism, consumerism, secularism; ecological crisis; genocide and other oppressive injustices in developing countries; increasing number of AIDS victims; war, inflated defense spending; exorbitant consumption and pollution; a media relatively divorced from principles of morality (or seemingly so); ignorance or purposeful rejection of our Creator and the connectedness of all creation; the possibility of nuclear annihilation and biochemical warfare? Don't these name only some of the general and the obvious? Do they overwhelm you? You may find the following to be both realistic and practical.

As an oblate or potential oblate, each of you will know best which issues to choose for service to God and others, and how best to address them. In your efforts to be authentic you will begin the process by looking deep within yourself. You know that you obviously serve God and others when you don't gossip, gripe, speak in unjust anger; when you don't lie, cheat, hold grudges, refuse to forgive, judge unjustly; in other words, when you keep God's commandments and continue your Benedictine values of personal transformation. You can always extend yourself in service to others by visiting the lonely, the sick, the undesirables, by really *listening* to them and being a caring presence. You can remember that God is in each person and every human being is precious in God's sight. Ask yourself how you can assist the homeless, the addicted, the depressed, and victims of violence? Can you serve your parish, school, youth center/groups? Could you help someone find a job, work for Habitat for Humanity? Will you become involved politically and be a vocal advocate for justice, peace, environmentally sound policies? Are you aware of and active in groups that address poverty, elder abuse, child abuse, abortion, health insurance issues, family, addiction, violence, hunger, environmental issues, justice, peace, equality? You can also investigate what societies and organizations your church sponsors and promotes and become actively involved with the needy through that channel.

Wherever and however you choose to serve, let it be done with genuine care, selflessness, and love. True service should really be *love in action*. Local, national, and global events keep reminding us that we exist as part of various communities and must reach out to others. Albert Einstein said: "Every day I remind myself that my inner and outer life are based on the labors of other men, living and dead, and that I must exert myself in order to give in the same measure as I have received and am still receiving." Every human person is connected to others in some way. We inherited a civilization based on the efforts and labors of others. We Americans enjoy freedom in a country whose Declaration of Independence accords each person the right to life, liberty, and the pursuit of happiness. We have received a mandate from the living God whose incarnate Son set out our task: "Love the Lord your God with your whole heart and soul and your neighbor as yourself" (see Matt 22:37-39).

Charles Peguy said: "When we come to the end of our pilgrimage and reach heaven, God will ask, 'Where are the others?'" Benedictine spirituality provides and asks that we become nourished by our prayer life and our ever-deepening personal relationship with God through the Eucharist, *lectio*, the Divine Office, and personal prayer, and that we then try each day to *live* it in our communities and ministries. The monastic and the oblate are asked to achieve a marriage of contemplation and action, to be people of prayer and strong morality, and to be actors for social justice in compassion and love.

James of Sacred Scripture invites us: "Be doers of the word, and not merely hearers who deceive themselves. . . . Religion that is pure and undefiled before God, the Father, is this: to care for orphans and widows in their distress, and to keep oneself unstained by the world" (Jas 1:22, 27). He continues: "What good is it, my brothers and sisters, if you say you have faith but do not have works? Can faith save you? If a brother or sister is naked and lacks daily food, and one of you says to them, 'Go in peace, keep warm, and eat your fill' and yet you do not supply their bodily needs, what is the good of that? So faith by itself, if it has no works, is dead" (Jas 2:14-17). Saint Bede the Venerable reminds us: "He alone loves the Creator perfectly who manifests a pure love for his neighbor." In his gospel, Saint John states: "I give you a new commandment, that you love one another" (John 13:34). "You received without payment; give without payment" (Matt 10:8). You will find so many more passages in the Bible regarding service and love in action that as you do your sacred reading and *lectio* you may want to write them in your journal as reminders.

Benedict was steeped in Sacred Scripture and the Rule; he quotes it freely and frequently. As you read the Rule you will find that the themes of love of God and service in love to your neighbor come through clearly. "Relieve the lot of the poor . . . *visit the sick*. . . . Go to help the troubled" (RB 4.14, 16, 18). Justice, rights, truth, peace are addressed. Concern for the needs of all and service to all, regardless of creed, sex, race, age, nationality, social status, gifts, are the province of monastics and oblates who would live Benedictine spirituality. "Let them prefer nothing whatever to Christ, and may he bring us all together to everlasting life" (RB 72.11)

CHAPTER 4

History of the Oblate Movement

General History of the Oblate Movement

It is difficult to write even a general minihistory of the Benedictine oblate movement because there is not a *single* thread that leads from the sixth century to the present. The definitive history has yet to be written but one can gather important data from cartularies and other historical sources including the Rule of Benedict itself. The following highlights of the phenomenon are but an effort to capture and share *some threads* of a concept and practice that goes back to the time of Benedict himself.

Oblation: Origins to the Nineteenth Century

Chapter 59 in the Rule makes it quite clear that in the sixth century, Saint Benedict was accepting even very young children offered to the monastery by their parents.

> If a member of the nobility offers his son to God in the monastery, and the boy himself is too young, the parents draw up the document . . . then, at the presentation of the gifts, they wrap the document itself and the boy's hand in the altar cloth. That is how they offer him. . . . Poor people do the same. (RB 59.1-2, 7)

Note that Benedict accepted the children of both the rich and the poor. The above information about child oblation is among the earliest we have concerning the "offering" of children to Benedict's monastery, although according to Saint Gregory the Great's *Life and*

Miracles of St. Benedict, boys were already offered to him (before he wrote the Rule) while he was at Subiaco. Referring to Benedict's time at Subiaco, Gregory writes:

> As Benedict's influence spread over the surrounding country-side because of his signs and wonders, a great number of men gathered around him to devote themselves to God's service. Christ blessed his work and before long he had established twelve monasteries there, with an abbot and twelve monks in each of them. There were a few other monks whom he kept with him since he felt that they still needed his personal guidance.
>
> It was about this time that pious noblemen from Rome first came to visit the saint and left their sons with him to be schooled in the service of God. Thus Euthicius brought his son Maurus, and senator Tertullus, Placid, both very prom-ising boys. Maurus, in fact, who was a little older, had already acquired solid virtue and was soon very helpful to his saintly master. But Placid was still only a child.[1]

While the practice of child oblation did not completely cease until around the twelfth century, the issues regarding the age of the child and whether or not the initial oblation was binding for life were debated throughout the ensuing centuries. Parental oblation of children was generally held to bind the child to the monastic state for life, and this position had been upheld by popes. The question was troublesome because of the difference of opinion concerning whether the child who had been given by the parents in oblation could disavow that commitment when she or he reached puberty and leave the monastery.

Abbé Deroux, Penelope Johnson, and other writers remind us that in early Christian history and in the Middle Ages, the child, male or female, was considered to be fully under family control. Family interests superseded those of the individual.[2] Several synods and councils addressed the issue of child oblation but Derek Smith says that, in practice, infant oblation continued until the twelfth century.[3] By the 1100s, legal schools taught that a valid act of profes-sion could not be made before puberty. It is possible that individual monasteries ended the acceptance of children earlier than the twelfth century. Smith notes that the capitulary of Aix-la-Chapelle, for example, held that to be valid a child oblation had to be confirmed by the oblate upon reaching the age of reason.[4] General church legislation on the matter came out of the Council of Trent (1545), which set sixteen years as the minimum age of profession.

Since the practice of child oblation may be puzzling and even offensive to contemporaries, it is important to address at least some of the reasons for its existence. The donation of a child to a monastery could have occurred for economic reasons. If the family was large, donating one or several children could relieve the family's financial worries and keep the children's inheritance in the parents' hands.[5] While Johnson focuses primarily on girls and women, she acknowledges that boys were also "disposed of in accord with family strategies."[6] She suggests that sometimes a child who might be a burden in secular society was given to the monastery. As examples she cites the disabled, the simpleminded, the poor, and especially in regard to females, the homely.[7] Johnson's focus is on religious women in the eleventh through thirteenth centuries in northern France. She gives specific examples of child oblation that help to clarify the rationale for this custom, concluding that: "The decision to give a child to a monastery was a choice to donate something of worth to God, thereby benefiting the souls of parents or guardians who offered the child for oblation."[8] She states: "At the heart of secular strategies for sending members into monasteries was a profound belief in the spiritual efficacy of monastic suffrages."[9]

Various forms of lay association with monasteries existed throughout the centuries. Terminology for similar types of such association might vary somewhat depending on different monasteries, countries, or centuries. Any attempt at accuracy regarding the terms used for adult oblates and the century in which the terms were first used is indeed a challenge whose details are not within the scope of this book. It is difficult because some terms that indicated lay brothers, adult oblates, and lay affiliates of monasteries may be synonymous. One source claims that from the seventh century onward, the word "oblate" was also used for *conversi, devoti, donati,* and *commissi* who looked after the material interests of the monastery.[10]

Elsewhere it is suggested that the term "oblate" referring to adults may not have been used before the eleventh century. In the ninth century the term "confratres" appears. Many monasteries probably had "confratres" before the eleventh century, which is witnessed to by a monk who wrote: "There are a great many of the faithful, both poor and rich, who request confraternity with us. We give unto all of them participation in whatever good is done in our monastery, be it by prayer or almsgiving. Let us make special prayer for them, both while they live and after their death."[11]

The name *conversi* was applied to monks who entered the monastery as adults, but it also applied to lay brothers. In monasteries from the seventh to ninth centuries there were *conversi* attached to the monasteries as a result of their donations and thus called *donati*. They did not take vows but were considered members of the community.[12] Deroux finds that, from at least the ninth century, some *donati* lived in the monastery and some were nonresidents. There were also people who were connected to monasteries in a spiritual way but could not live with the community because of their position or for socioeconomic reasons. They did not seek nor expect any financial gain, so the connection to the monastery had a certain spiritual dimension. The Holy Roman Emperor Henry II (973–1024), patron of oblates, an oblate of Saint Viton and Saint Vanne in Verdun, and King Philip I of France, an oblate of Cluny, are examples in point. History conveys that abbeys frequently had patrons who were a mixed blessing since they "both helped and harassed the nuns or monks under their protection."[13] These patrons gave monasteries direct gifts of money, and/or land and offered them emotional support and even a type of protection.[14] Does this not sound like some form of at least potential "oblate" association?

Cluny, a Benedictine monastery at its height from ca. AD 927–1109, had a monastic *familia* that "typically consisted of monks, monk-novices and several categories of lay affiliates under oblation who lived in the cloister and wore monastic habit."[15] Smith states: "Adult oblates living in monastic habit and in cloister, as an integral part of the monastic *familia*, were variously called *oblati conversi, oblati barbati, oblati illiterati, idiotae*, and a variety of other terms."[16]

Smith refers to *matricularii* as those laypeople who seem to have been drawn from certain lay prayer communities (*fraternitates*) that surrounded the monastery. These were supposedly in cloister under a form of oblation, wore a habit, and conducted business affairs for the monastery. In Judith Sutera's translation of Deroux she refers to *matricularii* as those who seemed to have lived at the monastery, kept a "quasi-monastic observance," lived in common, and perhaps had a tonsure or wore a distinctive garment.[17] Sutera reports that Deroux's classification of *donati* or *oblati* included those who offered their own will along with donations of goods.[18]

By the eleventh century, Abbot William of Hirschau gave some clarification of the oblate state by defining some oblates as interns or regular oblates who lived in the monastery and submitted to its discipline but did not make formal vows, and secular oblates who lived "in the world" but were affiliated with the monastery. Secular oblates promised obedience and sometimes also chastity "and made over a part or the whole of their possessions to the monastery either immediately or by way of legacy."[19]

Monastic life had suffered from interference by lay lords, the alienation of property, and the incursion of barbaric tribes. The attempted reforms in the tenth century called for a more strict following of the Rule of Benedict, freedom for monastic communities to choose their own leaders without lay interference, a greater fidelity to Liturgy of the Hours, and solemn celebration of the liturgy.[20] Numbered among the oblates at this time was the Holy Roman Emperor, Henry II. During Henry's time monasteries were cultural, educational, and economic centers as well as spiritual/religious ones. They had employees, servants, retirees, friends, and patrons. Henry's association with many monastic communities was multidimensional. He was "instrumental in reforming many monasteries," had abbots as his advisers, appointed some abbots, and gave generously to many of the monasteries.[21]

As the future unraveled, monasticism went into decline and disrepute chiefly due to drastic changes in societal and cultural Europe. One need only read the history of abbeys (e.g., the ninth through the nineteenth centuries) to understand the effects of society, politics, economics, and culture on the Catholic Church and, concomitantly, on monastic life. The Hundred Years' War (1337–1453) was devastating and it spawned brigands, pillaging, and rampant, random killing. It resulted in a type of anarchy that did little for monastic discipline. Some monasteries were led by nonresident and secular abbots.[22] In the 1340s the bubonic plague (the Black Death) swept across Europe, killing hundreds of thousands, depopulating monasteries, and obviously disrupting monastic life. Also, during these years, the Catholic Church itself was in turmoil. Thomas Bokenkotter claims that in Italy and Germany, the strife between the pope and emperor along with the "Great Schism" in the church, with three men claiming to be pope, "brought monasticism to a low ebb."[23] As monasticism went in these times, so too did the oblates.

Smith states that besides the above factors there were the following that contributed to monasticism's decline/nadir. He claims that monasteries/monastics were: (1) "spiritually weakened by the loss of the primacy of prayer in their way of life"; (2) "encumbered by elaborate liturgical developments inimical to the simplicity and humility of the traditional ethos of monastic culture"; and (3) "shackled by landed wealth" and "hamstrung by political allegiances to the monarchs and nobility of Europe."[24] To these, Smith adds the factor of the polarization of theology and traditional monastic spirituality. He decries the fact that monasticism "almost lost its priceless heritage of meditative prayer in its re-ordered priorities and in its secular entanglements."[25]

Despite the setbacks during these troubled times there were rays of hope. An example in point is Saint Frances of Rome (1384–1440), patroness of oblates, who managed to live a life of courage and faith. She founded an association of women oblates who were attached to the Benedictine Monastery of Santa Maria Nuova in Rome. The group of women later became the Benedictine Oblate Congregation of Tor de' Specchi, which was approved by Pope Eugene IV on July 4, 1433. These laywomen lived in the world and basically led the life of a religious through prayer and good works but did not make formal vows.

Gradually, through the centuries, some of the church's governing ecclesiastics had become extremely worldly. They had political power, accumulated material possessions, and held privileged positions in public life, and because they were also territorial princes, many bishops and abbots might even be considered secular rulers. Because of this and their love of luxury, many clergy were scorned by the people even though many laypeople themselves may have lived lives of immorality and religious indifference.

Since monasteries, and by association their oblates, were seriously affected by church, political, and societal issues, it is appropriate at this time to readdress the Great Schism of the Popes (1378–1417) and remember that it not only affected monasticism adversely but also the prestige and even influence of the papacy. The authority of the Holy See had been eroding through either its occupants and/or the secular princes. There was need for spiritual reform of the church in general. The nobility and "many secular rulers became bishops or abbots in order to control the Church and receive its revenues."[26] Attempted reforms of administrative abuses of the Papal Curia were not thorough. Civil authorities had been given many occasions to interfere in purely ecclesiastical affairs and often secular governments and civil powers sought to control church matters. Materialism continued to make inroads, morality was eroding, and with the supernatural life receiving less interest, monasteries declined (and with them the lay associations). Simony prevailed and "some secular rulers purchased the right to hold two or more Church offices."[27] These bishops did not care for their people. "Training for the lower clergy was lax, preaching was neglected, and such worldliness as concubinage was again commonplace. . . . Many monks lived outside the cloisters, while those within became increasingly attached to material life."[28]

Reform had been called for and achieved on certain levels, but a general renewal including that of Rome itself was needed. It did not come and soon the Reformation provoked the dissolution of monasteries on Europe's mainland and in England. Ideas indirectly flowing from Martin Luther's 1517 theses gave secular authorities the impetus to appropriate ecclesiastical property and dispose of it at will. Henry VIII's break with Rome and self-appointment as judge in ecclesiastical affairs gave him supposed power to act to gain more lands for himself and the gentry. The dissolution of England's monasteries occurred from 1536 to 1540.

The failure of spiritual reform at this time could have stemmed from a climate of financial excesses in the papacy as well as factions within the hierarchy that emphasized external rather than internal spiritual values.[29] Around this time, from about the middle of the fifteenth century onward, the popes were also preoccupied with the Renaissance and its humanism. While there were streams of renewal in the Catholic Church, ordinary Catholics were generally untouched by them and did not understand the basic truths of the Catholic faith because sound teaching from priests and bishops was "either rare or nonexistent."[30]

The Protestant Reformation (c. 1517–1650) splintered Christianity but appeared to ignite a more diligent effort of reform and renewal within the Catholic Church. The Catholic Reformation (c. 1500–1650)[31] was spurred by the renewal of existing religious orders and the founding of new ones. The Council of Trent (1545–63) might be termed the Reform Council. It clarified and defined what the Catholic Church taught, corrected many of the abuses, and established a diocesan seminary system to form and educate priests. Catholics were encouraged to receive Holy Communion frequently and the sacrament of penance more often. Benediction and Forty Hours services encouraged devotion to Jesus in the Blessed Sacrament. This age also produced many great mystics and activist/missionary saints.[32] In general it has been stated that the Protestant Reformation had devastating effects on the Benedictines who were practically obliterated throughout northwestern Europe. "The vigorous new life in the Benedictine family was confronted by Protestantism in the sixteenth century. In England, Scotland, Denmark, Sweden, Norway, Iceland, Holland, and much of Germany monasticism was swept away. In Switzerland, France, and Belgium it endured a cruel ordeal."[33]

It is obviously simplistic to try to address or condense whole periods of history in these short paragraphs. The reader is hereby referred to access the many historical sources for details and complete accuracy. Suffice it to say that as the Benedictine Order went, so did the oblates of Saint Benedict. The Benedictines' experience of religious wars, suppression, and ejection from their monasteries did little to stabilize or promote the oblate state during these years.

As we move into the era of the "Modern World" (ca. 1650–1900) we encounter the Age of Enlightenment, including rationalism, science and technology, leading to the Industrial Revolution, political upheaval due to new forms of government, and the exclusion of religion from many aspects of public society, which could be termed "secularization." Despite intellectual wars and theological disputes, the average layperson could still find a home in the Catholic Church with a normal life of prayer and devotion.[34] At this time the spiritual life of the Catholic Church spawned the Trappist Order, which is guided by the Rule of Benedict (1664); the Passionist Order (1725); and the Redemptorists (1732). Yet, during the eighteenth century, the prestige and influence of the Catholic Church reached a low point and there was again a need for renewal and reform in Catholic religious orders.

It is not our intent to follow the fate of monasteries in each country, but some examples should suffice to help the reader understand why oblate associations have suffered in the past. Maybe the seventeenth century could show a certain spirit of Catholic revival, but by the eighteenth century the Catholic Church and its monasteries received another powerful blow at the hands of the French Revolution. The church was a large landowner in France and received revenues from its tenants and tithes. By the time of the Revolution members of the nobility held senior church positions with wealthy revenues while many priests in rural areas or small communities lived in poverty. Social and economic grievances increased among the people and the church began to be perceived by many to be extremely interested in preserving its wealth and privileges rather than focusing on spiritual things. On July 11, 1789, the populace sacked the monasteries. On November 2, 1789, ecclesiastical goods were confiscated to the state; on February 13, 1790, monastic vows were forbidden, and religious orders of men and women were suppressed.

In summary, fueled by the Enlightenment, rationalism, and absolute monarchies, there was widespread suppression of abbeys in the eighteenth century. "Benedictine oblates were more or less numerous in European monasteries until about 1780."[35] When the number of monasteries was greatly reduced it was natural that oblature diminished.

While anti-Catholicism, anticlericalism, and persecution of Roman clerics and monastic orders continued at this time, some resentments against the church even took the form of a type of atheism. There was desecration of churches and some cathedrals, and abbeys and monasteries were totally destroyed. Things in France did not improve much during the Napoleonic era, which continued to forbid the practice of the Catholic faith until the concordat with the Holy See in 1802. This concordat made the public practice of the Catholic religion once again legal in France and allowed that some restitution be made for the extreme damage that the Revolution had caused to ecclesiastical property.[36]

It is not within the scope of this book to pursue the matter in more detail. Some of the examples given will allow the reader to deduce why such things as the Hundred Years' War, the Reformation, the French Revolution, and the Napoleonic Era were hardly conducive to monasticism in general and lay association with monasteries in particular.

In Europe, throughout the nineteenth century "the Catholic Church lost thousands of acres of land and countless monasteries and other houses through the secularization (government takeover) of Church property."[37] The ending of political alliance between the church and state in Europe helped lead the Catholic Church to focus on its *spiritual* mission. After some of the havoc endured through the centuries, the beginning of the nineteenth century in France, for example, saw the building of new monasteries and convents. One of the blessings of the nineteenth century was the establishment of new religious orders and the revitalization of established ones. Some suppressed abbeys were restored and there was a revitalization of monasticism, including the founding of Benedictine abbeys in America. The reinstatement of oblature followed. In 1898 the status of oblates was canonically established by Pope Leo XIII. The statutes and Rules of the Secular Oblates of Saint Benedict were officially approved in a decree issued by the Sacred Congregation of Bishops and Regulars in 1904 and, after some alterations and additions, were confirmed by the Sacred Congregation of Religious in 1927.

Oblation: America 1900–2000

For our purposes we will now follow the monastic life and the oblate movement from Europe across the Atlantic to America.

Abbot Boniface Wimmer, OSB, from the Bavarian Abbey of Metten, came to the United States in 1846 and founded Saint Vincent's

Archabbey in Latrobe, Pennsylvania. By 1865 he was speaking to Abbot Hugo Lang of Metten about his desire "to bring about some sort of third order of St. Benedict into which lay people of both sexes can be admitted."[38] The same source also declares: "An old certificate of Oblation states that the 'Institute of Secular Oblates of the Benedictine Order' was introduced to the United States with papal approval by Abbot Boniface on August 6, 1865" (53). Though the archabbey archives have no record of oblations until August 1917, the first *Manual for Benedictine Oblates* was published by the archabbey in 1898.

In his preface to the Saint John's Abbey (Collegeville, Minnesota) *Manual for Oblates of St. Benedict*, written in 1937, Abbot Alcuin Deutsch of Saint John's refers to the Saint Vincent *Manual* of 1898 and to the 1923 and 1932 editions. In the Saint John's *Manual* Abbot Alcuin states:

> The Institute of the Secular Oblates of St. Benedict was reorganized at the request of the Right Reverend Dom Hildebrand de Hemptinne, O.S.B., Abbot of the International Benedictine College of St. Anselm in Rome and Primate of the Benedictine Order. For this purpose he obtained two Pontifical documents: a) A Brief of Leo XIII, dated June 17, 1898, in which many spiritual favors and privileges were granted to the Oblates: b) A Decree of the Sacred Congregation of Bishops and Regulars, dated July 23, 1904, approving the Statutes and Rules for Secular Oblates of St. Benedict, which had been submitted to the Holy See by the Abbot Primate. After a few slight alterations and additions had been made in 1927, this new edition of the Statutes and Rules was again approved by a Rescript of the Sacred Congregation of Religious, on March 24, 1927.[39]

Saint John's Abbey in Collegeville, Minnesota, was founded in 1856. Interest in the oblate movement was already strong at Saint John's in 1877, because among the abbey's first publications "was a seven-page pamphlet composed in both German and English by Abbot Alexius [Edelbrock, second Abbot of Saint John's Abbey] in 1877 to foster the institute of Oblates of St. Benedict among students, parishioners and friends of the abbey."[40]

In *Worship and Work*, Colman Barry cites that the oblate program "had been revived in the United States in 1894 by Archabbot Leander Schnerr of St. Vincent" (p. 261). He refers to the fact that Abbot Alcuin (Deutsch) and Prior Alfred (Mayer) of Saint John's Abbey fostered an interest in the oblate program in 1925, and that Abbot Alcuin received sixty oblates there on the feast of Saint Benedict, March 21, 1925. The Solemnity of Saint Benedict, July 11, was chosen as annual Oblates' Day at Saint John's. The movement began to attract students and alumni of Saint John's University, friends, and other laity, and soon a director of oblates was appointed. By January 22, 1927, a monthly paper was first issued and a lending library of spiritual books made available. The Saint John's newsletter was titled simply *Oblate*. In 1956 the Saint John's oblate membership totaled sixteen hundred. Among that total were women students at the neighboring College of Saint Benedict who had made their oblation at the college but had to be affiliated with Saint John's because they could not yet have affiliation with Benedictine women monasteries. That condition would soon change.

While each Benedictine monastery in America has its own enlightening history of lay oblation, in the interest of continuity we have chosen to continue to follow the sequence of events that led to the establishment of the oblate program at Saint Benedict's Monastery, the Benedictine women's monastery in Saint Joseph, Minnesota. It offers a clear example of oblation evolution in America and gives the reader a clear picture of a monastery's relational connections to and procedural issues regarding administrative aspects of the central authority of the Catholic Church in Rome.

History of the Oblates of Saint Benedict's Monastery: An Example of the Oblate Evolution in America

Saint Benedict's Monastery in Saint Joesph, Minnesota, was founded in 1857. For many years, it was known as the Convent of Saint Benedict or Saint Benedict's Convent. The name was changed to Saint Benedict's Monastery on March 23, 1996, and this name will be used thoughout this text, regardless of the time frame being discussed.

The oblate movement at Saint Benedict's appears to have begun in the 1930s with Sister Alfreda Zierdan, OSB. In her oral interview, Sister Alfreda speaks of getting the oblates started and working with them at the College of Saint Benedict where she taught. The College of Saint Benedict is an all-women's college on the same campus as Saint Benedict's Monastery. Sister Alfreda also spoke of the oblate situation as being a "gradual and optional movement" and reminisced that she first became interested in the oblates when she went to Notre Dame.[41] During these years, the College of Saint Benedict also had a League of the Divine Office (named after Saint Frances of Rome, patroness of oblates) whose members would recite some hours of the Divine Office daily. Sister Alfreda was instrumental in promoting this league and there may have been some relationship in her mind between this group and those who had become oblates. Sister Alfreda also shared the oblate letters produced by the monks of Saint John's Abbey by posting them on the Sodality bulletin board.[42] Any person who became an oblate at the College of Saint Benedict in these early years either went to Saint John's Abbey to make her final oblation before the abbot or signed her oblation document on the altar of Sacred Heart Chapel at Saint Benedict's Monastery but was still affiliated with Saint John's Abbey.

Sister Alfreda was undoubtedly the informal director of oblates at the College of Saint Benedict until she went to the Bahamas in 1951. At this point it appears that Sister Joanne Muggli, OSB, succeeded her in this position at the college. During these years the majority of oblates came from the college although some lay employees, and no doubt students' parents and other friends, had also shown interest.[43] There is definite evidence that Sister Joanne was working with the oblates at the College of Saint Benedict at least by 1954. She held that position until 1972.

The letter dated January 15, 1962, from Mother (Prioress) Henrita Ostendorf, OSB, of Saint Benedict's Monastery to Abbot Primate Benno Gut, OSB, brought about an important change to the oblate situation at Saint Benedict's. Mother Henrita inquired whether it was possible "to have oblates make their final oblation for a convent of Benedictine sisters and be affiliated with a convent rather than with a monastery." She also asked: "If so, what steps would we need to take to transfer the affiliation of our Oblates from St. John's Abbey to our convent?" In response, Abbot Primate Gut, in a letter dated January 31, 1962, sent Mother Henrita a rescript from the Sacred Congregation of Religious which affirmed that convents of Benedictine nuns could affiliate oblates to the convent. The abbot primate also offered to ask the Sacred Congregation of Religious for a declaration that the transfer of oblates was included in Number 96 of the *Lex Propria*, which permitted the abbot primate to transfer the stability of monks and nuns from one monastery to another "even in different Congregations."

Abbot Primate Gut's letter of February 24, 1962, to Mother Henrita confirms that he received the authorization to transfer oblates from one monastery to another even in diverse congregations. He then lists the following steps necessary for transfer of stability: "1. A letter from the oblate stating his or her desire to transfer. 2. A letter from the Superior of the monastery '*a quo*' (in this case, Saint John's) consenting to the transfer. 3. A letter from the Superior of the monastery '*ad quod*' (your convent) stating that the Superior and Council (or whoever passes on the admission of oblates) are willing to accept the candidate." He adds: "When I have all this for each candidate I will issue a document of transfer for each." The abbot primate concludes by thanking Mother Henrita "for being the stimulus or occasion for me to obtain the faculty which I think will be much used in the future."

By August 20, 1962, Mother Henrita wrote a letter to the prioresses of the federation, informing them of all that had transpired regarding affiliation permission and transfer of oblation. In this letter she includes the following information for clarification purposes, stating:

> That convents definitely may receive Oblates, just as monasteries do. That all the privileges, indulgences, etc. which attach to Oblates of monasteries pertain with equal validity to Oblates who may become affiliated with convents. That any priest may be asked to perform the ceremonies of investiture and profession, and that this priest may be designated (or asked) to do this by the Mother of the convent receiving the Oblates.

She concludes the letter by stating that she feels this permission is a great blessing for Benedictine convents. Her final statement reads:

"We could make it part of our apostolate to inculcate in lay people the spirituality of our holy Father Benedict who has so much to offer not only to monks and nuns but to all people."

Almost immediately, in a letter she wrote on May 10, 1962, Sister Joanne Muggli, the oblate director at Saint Benedict's Monastery, informed the oblates who had been invested at Saint Benedict's but had had to be affiliated with Saint John's Abbey, of the newly obtained permission. Among other things she states: "We consider it a great privilege to be able to affiliate Oblates with our community. It unites us on a deeper, more spiritual plane with students, alumnae, lay employees, and friends with whom we have been associated. It is really according to the mind of Saint Benedict to have the lay people associated with us in our work considered as our Oblates sharing in the work and prayer of the Sisters." After sharing the news that fourteen college girls were invested with the Benedictine scapular and three made their final oblation for Saint Benedict's Convent (Monastery), she speaks of the other laywomen who have been invested. She states: "We may receive both men and women as Oblates." Sister Joanne then offers the oblates the choice of maintaining their stability at Saint John's Abbey or transferring their affiliation to Saint Benedict's.

In Sister Joanne's oblate newsletter of September 1, 1962, she welcomes "as part of our family" those who have transferred affiliation to Saint Benedict's Convent (Monastery), appreciating the fact that they can now "share in the work and prayer of the Sisters in a more intimate way." At this time thirty-five had completed the transfer and "a number more" were in the process.

It was planned that a Mass would be offered for oblates each month. Those oblates on campus planned to have breakfast together after the Mass, accompanied by a short reading from the lives of Benedictine saints.

On September 2, 1962, the first group of oblates to be affiliated with Saint Benedict's Monastery from Saint Raphael's Home in Saint Cloud were invested at Saint Raphael's Home Chapel.

A missive in rough draft was written in the summer of 1962 by Mother Henrita. Though never finalized or sent, it was intended to inform the Sisters of Saint Benedict's Monastery about some of the specifics regarding permission for oblate affiliation. Instead of writing to all the sisters "on mission" concerning the matter, she decided to share more information with them at the July 1962, chapter meeting. In the rough draft she spoke of the need to plan for specific benefits for "our oblates." She said: "Since Oblates are considered as part of the Benedictine family, they share in our work and prayer. . . . In time, we will hold regular meetings and perhaps have an Oblate day sometime during the summer. We also hope to establish a lending library for Oblates since they are encouraged to do spiritual reading." Mother Henrita also spoke of a monthly Mass offered specifically for the oblates.

Sister Joanne Muggli continued as the director of the oblates at Saint Benedict's Monastery from the 1950s to the summer of 1972. Her newsletters usually contained a paragraph from the prioress, with content ranging from convent and college news, social and church-related events, what to pray for worldwide, and many other interesting news bites. By September 7, 1972, Sister Mary Anthony Wagner was writing the oblate newsletter. Sister Mary Anthony held the position of director until her death on September 18, 2002.

Sister Mary Anthony was thoroughly dedicated to the oblate movement and throughout her years as director, there were as many as twelve hundred people who received her newsletter. In her oral history, Sister Mary Anthony describes the typical contents of her newsletters as follows: (1) the first part is formative and usually deals with the Rule or season of the liturgy, (2) the second part includes readings for the Sunday liturgy and prayers, (3) the third part would be news about the community and news from the oblates themselves, and (4) the ending would again have a spiritual thrust.

Sister Mary Anthony recalled that the North American Association of Benedictine Oblate Directors first included women at its 1980 meeting at Saint Anselm's Abbey, Manchester, New Hampshire.[44] In 1984 Sister Mary Anthony was elected coordinator of the association and "the directors' confidence in her leadership was quickly confirmed, for she was re-elected to a second two-year term in 1986."[45]

During Sister Mary Anthony's leadership, the oblates of Saint Benedict's Monastery received nine newsletters a year. Oblate discussion groups were formed for three different areas: Minneapolis / Saint Paul, MN; Saint Joseph, MN; and Saint Benedict's Senior Community Center in Saint Cloud, Minnesota.

During the annual Oblate Renewal Day the oblates attended meals and Eucharist with the sisters, then, at prayers in the monastic oratory, candidates were received and testimonials given. Renewal Day also included guest speakers, a book sale, door prizes, and entertainment.

In the mid-1970s, Saint Benedict's Monastery had two resident oblates. One joined the Benedictine community by becoming a religious. The resident program was discontinued in 1975, but was resumed in 2009. The most recent oblate in residence lived at Saint Benedict's Monastery in 2011.

At the time of Sister Mary Anthony's death there were over seven hundred listed active oblates of Saint Benedict's Monastery, Saint Joseph, MN, and an unknown number of less active or inactive ones spread across the United States and also located in the Ukraine, Canada, England, Puerto Rico, the Bahamas, Australia, Korea, Mexico, Costa Rica, and Germany. Saint Benedict's Monastery and Saint John's Abbey hosted the North American Directors of Benedictine Oblates and oblates from July 27 to August 1, 2001. The event brought 134 people to these campuses. This was one of the last huge events that Sister Mary Anthony organized as director of oblates. On August 1, 2001, Renewal Day at Saint Benedict's Monastery, she spoke with great enthusiasm of the vitality and spirit of Benedict experienced among the oblates. Soon after these events her health began to fail and she died on September 18, 2002.

The oblate programs at Saint Benedict's Monastery and Saint John's Abbey in Minnesota continue with dynamic vitality to this day. The number of laypeople seeking to live Benedictine spirituality gives evidence of the human longing for God in our very busy, consumer-driven, materialistic culture. After reading the above, it must be obvious that oblation in the twentieth and beginning of the twenty-first centuries has seen a dramatic revival. Many monasteries in America have seen an increase in numbers of oblates as many God-seekers continue to investigate Benedictine spirituality and apply to the oblate programs throughout the country. These monasteries and their offerings can be easily accessed online.

The Importance of the Laity in the Work of the Church and the World

As we have seen, one who decides to become a Benedictine oblate chooses to live an intentional and hopefully intense Christian spiritual life, imbued with the values of Benedictine spirituality and the Gospel on which it is based. The affirmation of the laity, the recognition and even definition, of their role in the church, in society, and the world is clearly presented in the documents of Vatican II. Benedictine oblates are a leaven for good and God in their vocation, career, geographical area of choice, in every area of society in which they are engaged. As such they are helping to fulfill what the council of Vatican II entrusts to them and asks of them in the following quoted documents. Do not be surprised at how valuable you are to the church and the world. You are the People of God with a special role to play for God's kingdom and creation.

As you read this section you will encounter language that is non-inclusive, not "politically correct." Please remember that the words are direct quotes from the translated documents. I decided not to constantly insert parenthetical additions of inclusive language in order that the text was not consistently interrupted. Knowing this, I hope that no one will take offense but will focus on the content instead, marveling at the importance of every human being in the eyes of God and the Vatican II authors.

While poring over the documents of Vatican II, one cannot help but be impressed by the many references to the importance of the laity in the life of the church. In Vatican II's Pastoral Constitution on the Church in the Modern World, we read that the laity have an active, distinctive role to play in the whole life of the church and are "called to be witnesses to Christ in all things in the midst of human society."[1] This theme is repeated in some form or another throughout the various relevant documents of Vatican II and will be referred to under each decree's specific title.

In *Lumen Gentium* (the Dogmatic Constitution on the Church), one of the key documents of the council, we read that the laity are sharers in the "priestly, prophetic, and kingly functions of Christ" (LG 31, p. 57). By virtue of their baptism and confirmation, all believers share in the general priesthood. The laity are the presence of the church in the world and work for its sanctification from within, making Christ known to others by a life "resplendent in faith, hope and charity" (LG 31, p. 58). This document emphasizes that "there is in Christ and in the Church no inequality on the basis of race or nationality, social condition or sex" (LG 32, p. 58). It states that pastors and the faithful "are bound to each other by mutual need" and continues thus: "The laity are called in a special way to make the Church present and operative in those places and circumstances where only through them can she become the salt of the earth" (LG 33, p. 59).

The laity are to be given every opportunity to participate in the saving work of the church according to their abilities and the needs of the times. They share in Christ's priestly function as all their works, prayers, and efforts become spiritual sacrifices acceptable to God through Jesus (see LG 34, p. 60). *Lumen Gentium* says that Christ continually fulfills his prophetic office "not only through the hierarchy who teach in His name and with His authority, but also through the laity" (LG 35, p. 61). The laity can be a living testimony to faith and the love of Christ in their daily family and social life. The laity are called to "assist one another to live holier lives even in their daily occupations" (LG 36, p. 62) to help the world achieve justice, charity, and peace. They are to be guided by a Christian conscience in every temporal affair, making an effort to harmonize their rights and duties as members of the church with those they have as members of human society.

The thirty-seventh article of *Lumen Gentium* states: "An individual layman, by reason of the knowledge, competence, or outstanding ability which he may enjoy, is permitted and sometimes even obliged to express his opinion on things which concern the good of the Church" (LG 37, p. 64). This should be done in prudence, courage, and truth "with reverence and charity toward those who by reason of their sacred office represent the person of Christ" (LG 37, p. 64). The laity are to pray for their pastors and be obedient to their teaching, and the pastors are to "recognize and promote the dignity as well as the responsibility of the layman in the Church," willingly making use "of his prudent advice" (LG 37, p. 64). The pastor is to "confidently assign duties to him (the layperson) in the service of the Church, allowing him freedom and room for action" (LG 37, p. 64–65). The suggestion to pastors continues: "Further, let them encourage the layman so that he may undertake tasks on his own initiative. Attentively in Christ, let them consider with fatherly love the projects, suggestions, and desires proposed by the laity. Furthermore, let pastors respectfully acknowledge that just freedom which belongs to everyone in this earthly city" (LG 37, p. 65)

This "familiar dialogue" between the laity and their pastors is to give the laity "a strengthened sense of personal responsibility, a renewed enthusiasm, a more ready application of their talents to the projects of their pastors." The pastors, "aided by the experience of the laity, can more clearly and more suitably come to decisions regarding spiritual and temporal matters" (LG 37, p. 65).

What we have just noted from *Lumen Gentium* lays a foundation for the council's *Apostolicam Actuositatem* (Decree on the Apostolate of the Laity), which states in the introduction: "The layman's apostolate derives from his Christian vocation, and the Church can never be without it" (AA 1, p. 489). No council before Vatican II had tried to state official teaching on the lay apostolate and laity's "co-responsibility for the mission of Christ in the Church and in the world."[2] It is the laypeople who have to "bring Christianity into the marketplace" because they are, as Paul VI said, the "bridge to the modern world."[3] Because this decree was written "wishing to intensify the apostolic activity of the People of God" (AA 1, p. 489), it deserves the type of study and reflection that cannot be addressed here. Instead, we will extrapolate some concepts that may be helpful in elucidating the layperson's role and value to the church.

This Decree on the Apostolate of the Laity reiterates what the Dogmatic Constitution on the Church has also expressed—namely, that "the laity, too, share in the priestly, prophetic, and royal office of Christ and therefore have their own role to play in the mission of the whole People of God in the Church and in the world" (AA 2, p. 491). The laity are to bring the Gospel and holiness to humankind, and bring their Christian influence into the realm of society and its institutions for the good and salvation of others. They are to be a leaven in the secular sphere of the world. The laity have the right and duty to use their God-given gifts in the church and in the world for the good of both. "The success of the lay apostolate depends upon the laity's living union with Christ" (AA 4, p. 493), and this life is nourished by the church's spiritual aids, especially the sacred liturgy, and by their performing their secular duties in union with Christ and with God's will. Among life's struggles laypeople are to find strength in hope and, impelled by divine charity, they express the true spirit of the beatitudes in their lives. The laity should seek to please God rather than men and are "neither depressed by the lack of temporal goods nor puffed up by their abundance" (AA 4, p. 494). They should highly esteem professional skill, civic spirit, family, and the virtues of honesty, sincerity, kindness, courage, and justice "without which there can be no true Christian life" (AA 4, p. 495).

This document affirms that everything that God made is good and has intrinsic value. It goes on to consider that among the elements of the temporal order are the good things of life and the prosperity of the family, culture, economic affairs, the arts and professions, political institutions, international relations, and "other matters of this kind," as well as their development and progress. All of these were created for the human person, for our welfare.

"The laity must take on the renewal of the temporal order as their own special obligation" (AA 7, p. 498). They must "seek the justice characteristic of God's kingdom" and apply Christian social action to "the whole temporal sphere, including culture" (AA 7, p. 498). They should practice the works of mercy wherever there is need and try to help eliminate the causes of societal ills as well as the effects. The synod considers these fields of action important: church communities, the family, youth, the social milieu, and national and international affairs. Subsequently there is this recognition: "Since in our times women have an ever more active share in the whole life of society, it is very important that they participate more widely also in the various fields of the Church's apostolate" (AA 9, p. 500).

The Decree on the Apostolate of the Laity then goes on to specify the types of action in which laypeople can participate in each field previously listed. Regarding the church, for example, the laity should participate in parish, diocesan, interparochial, interdiocesan, national, and international projects. Among the activities under the family apostolate, some of the following are listed: affirming the right and duty of parents and guardians to educate children in a Christian manner, seeing that attention is paid to the needs of the family in government policies, adoption of abandoned infants, hospitality to strangers, catechetical work, support of married couples and families involved in material and moral crises, help for the aged.

The social and political importance of youth in modern society is confirmed in this document. It acknowledges that if youth are imbued with the spirit of Christ, their zeal and energy are effective qualities for ministry to each other and the church. Adults should offer youth good example and balanced advice and assistance.

The social milieu comments begin thus:

> The apostolate of the social milieu, that is, the effort to infuse a Christian spirit into the mentality, customs, laws, and structures of the community in which a person lives, is so much the duty and responsibility of the laity that it can never be properly performed by others. In this area the laity can exercise the apostolate of like toward like. It is here that laymen add to the testimony of life the testimony of their speech; it is here in the arena of their labor, profession, studies, residence, leisure, and companionship that laymen have a special opportunity to help their brothers. (AA 13, p. 504)

Laypeople are reminded that "there are many persons who can hear the gospel and recognize Christ only through the laity who live near them" (AA 13, p. 505).

Regarding the national and international apostolates, the laity should recognize the sense of solidarity among all peoples. They should promote the common good and make their opinion felt "so that civil authority may act with justice, and laws may conform to moral precepts" (AA 14, p. 505).

Because this document states that there should be mutual esteem among all forms of the church's apostolate, it specifies that "the hierarchy should promote the apostolate of the laity, provide it with spiritual principles and support, direct the exercise of this apostolate to the common good of the Church, and attend to the preservation of doctrine and order" (AA 24, p. 513). In addition, "bishops, pastors of parishes, and other priests of both branches of the clergy should keep in mind that the right and duty to exercise the apostolate is common to all the faithful, both clergy and laity, and that the laity also have their own proper roles in building up the Church" (AA 25, p. 514). Religious brothers and sisters should also "devote themselves to promoting lay enterprises" (AA 25, p. 515).

Formation of laypeople for the apostolate should be well rounded and "adapted to the natural abilities and circumstances of each layperson" who should be an active member of his own society, not only "adjusted to its culture," but "well-informed about the modern world." The layperson should be spiritually formed and sensitive to the movement of the Holy Spirit and "learn how to view, judge, and do all things in the light of faith" (AA 29, p. 517). The layperson's instruction in theology, ethics, and philosophy should be adjusted to "differences of age, status, and natural talents" (AA 29, p. 517), and the integrity of the human personality must be considered always.

It seems relevant to interject here a reminder of the formation of the Benedictine oblate. You will recall that the Benedictine oblate moves through one to five years of candidacy in which she or he studies the Rule of Benedict along with contemporary interpretations and practical applications of it. The candidate prays the Liturgy of the Hours, practices *lectio divina*, and, depending on the monastery of the candidate's choice, will probably attend days of recollection, retreats, and show evidence of being engaged in some apostolic works of mercy or involvement in social justice issues. The candidate is also mentored and no doubt reads additional spirituality books. These and other growthful experiences continue and expand as the candidate moves into final commitment to the oblate way of life. Obviously the oblates are ideal people in the lay world to carry out the desires of Vatican II.

Returning to the Decree on the Apostolate of the Laity we read that existing aids for the layperson's apostolic endeavors include "study sessions, congresses, periods of recollection, spiritual exercises, frequent meetings, conferences, books, and periodicals" (AA 32, p. 520). In addition, to better develop the natural capacities of laymen and laywomen, young or adult, "centers of documentation and study not only in theology but also in anthropology, psychology, sociology, and methodology should be established for all fields of the apostolate" (AA 32, p. 520). This document then reiterates that laypeople are God's coworkers in the "Church's one apostolate, which must be constantly adapted to the new needs of the times" (AA 33, p. 521).

The Decree on the Church's Missionary Activity (*Ad Gentes*) suggests that groups be organized so that the lay apostolate "will be able to permeate the whole of society with the spirit of the gospel" (AG 15, p. 602). It states: "The Church has not been truly established, and is not yet fully alive, nor is it a perfect sign of Christ among men, unless there exists a laity worthy of the name working along with the hierarchy. For the gospel cannot be deeply imprinted on the talents, life, and work of any people without the active presence of laymen. Therefore, even in the very founding of a Church, the greatest attention is to be paid to raising up a mature Christian laity" (AG 21, pp. 610–11). Since they belong both to the church and civil society, "their main duty, whether they are men or women, is the witness which they are bound to bear to Christ by their life and works in the home, in their social group, and in their own professional circle" (AG 21, p. 611). They must be acquainted with their own national traditions and heal and preserve their culture, developing it in accordance with modern conditions, and finally perfecting it in Christ so the faith of Christ can start to permeate and transform the society in which they live. "Laymen cooperate in the Church's work of evangelization. As witness and at the same time as living instruments, they share in her saving mission" (AG 41, p. 628).

These Vatican II documents leave no doubt as to the importance of the laity to the church and the world. As oblates of Saint Benedict, laypeople bring a wealth of spiritual gifts and professional talent to a world in dire need of spiritual resuscitation. With their chosen Benedictine monastery as their spiritual home and support, the oblates' personal spiritual transformation and social impact can be the leaven for the modern world for which Christ and the church yearn.

A recent symposia on secularity and the Gospel addressed the issue of how Christian faith can thrive in a secular world. Among other things, it identified some of the present tensions of the ecclesial community. Some examples were: (1) the liberal in tension with the conservative, (2) the theological in tension with the devotional, (3) the liturgical in tension with the pastoral, (4) the prophetic in tension with institutional structures, (5) missionary in tension with maintenance, (6) denominational commitment in tension with ecumenism, and (7) being "set apart from" in tension with "being in identity with" the larger community.[4] These church-related issues are but "tip of the iceberg" material calling for lay involvement.

As Christians committed to bringing Christ and the Gospel to family life, local communities, and the national and international stage, oblates help sanctify the world from within. They are key role models and probably, as laypeople, the most effective missionaries because of their natural connection to secular social, economic, educational, political, and artistic life, in accord with what Vatican II documents suggest. They take Christ and Gospel values to wherever they live, worship, work, and play. They bring to whomever they contact the good news of the God who created us, loves us unconditionally, sent his Son, Jesus, into the world to show us how to live, how to be happy, how to overcome death and be saved. What a vital and superb vocation for a needy world!

Reflection

1. Summarize the value of the laity to the church and the world as stated in the Vatican II documents addressed above.

2. How can you bring the Gospel message to contemporary society without alienating people or watering down the message?

3. In what *specific* way does the Benedictine oblate carry out Vatican II's call to the laity?

4. Where in your life do you find society and culture indifferent to, or alienated from, God? From the church? From any institutionalized religion? Why has this happened? In what way can you address those issues to instigate a change in attitude or encourage open minds and hearts?

CHAPTER 6

The Oblate Program

How to Begin: The Entering Process

Any Christian man or woman seeking to enter an oblate program should contact the director of oblates or any member of his or her chosen Benedictine monastery. Information may also be obtained by contacting any present oblate of that monastery.

The period of formation through which a potential oblate passes is structured to help the person understand Benedictine spirituality, values, tradition, and heritage. It will also help the potential candidate grow in the knowledge of how to apply these aspects in daily life as he or she experiences it. Key components are the Rule of Benedict and prayer.

Discerning the Call

As you take stock of where you are in life do you feel that something is missing? In the best-case scenario you may have a successful career, a strong family life, and no financial worries, but you sense that you may be living a rather superficial life and that there is really more. In the worst-case scenario you are totally unhappy, constantly struggling with yourself and relationships, and wondering, "where is life's meaning?" In either case you may be ready to begin a spiritual journey. Each potential oblate will bring a personal history to the task of spiritual growth. If you are ready for more meaning to your life, you are probably bringing great potential to a deeper relationship with God. If you are ready to choose a guide for that relationship with God and a structured path toward integration of body, mind, and spirit, you can find it in the Rule of Benedict.

Saint Benedict offers a guide regarding relationships, material things, study, work, prayer, worship, and many other essentials of life. It will not be a "to do" list; instead, it offers an attitude toward daily life, a framework on which to build and live a full Christian life. If you want to start finding God in the persons and experiences/ events of your life; if you want to balance your work with prayer and take more time for quiet, for others, for God; if you want to grow in the fullness and joy of Christian life, be more attentive to God's word, whether in Scripture, other people, or liturgy; if you need strengthening of faith to face life's trials, perhaps God is calling you to become a Benedictine oblate.

Steps in Oblate Formation

Conditions for Becoming an Oblate

Period of inquiry. This consists of one to several months of dialogue between the person inquiring and the director of oblates. During this time the person inquiring is given information about the oblate way of life and the oblate program at his or her chosen monastery.

Becoming a candidate. Upon completion of the period of inquiry, the interested person would take the next step in the program, which is that of becoming a candidate. At the ritual of reception, the oblate candidate will probably receive a copy of the Rule of Benedict and a medal of Saint Benedict or something similar, depending on the monastery's choice. During the first year of candidacy, the candidate is accompanied by a sponsor who supports the candidate on his or her spiritual journey through mutual sharing regarding the Benedictine tradition and Benedictine spirituality.

Period of candidacy. During this one- to five-year period, the oblate candidate is introduced to the oblate way of life. The primary focus of this period is the Rule of Benedict along with other practices to be determined by the candidate from specific options given. As stated, the candidate will be accompanied and supported by a sponsor (a religious member or another oblate) during the first year of candidacy.

Rite of Acceptance for Final Commitment. The time for receiving the Final Commitment of oblate candidates is decided by each specific monastery. By a certain date of the year in which an oblate candidate is ready to make her or his Final Commitment, the candidate will, for example, probably write a summary, stating:

1. How she or he has grown as an oblate candidate and has undertaken the practices required by the monastery's oblate program (plus other recommended ones, if desired)

2. How she or he hopes to continue to grow closer to Christ as a full oblate

The request will then be reviewed by the prioress, the director of oblates, and the candidate's sponsor. The candidate will be informed of their decision.

Oblation

Retreat prior to Rite of Final Commitment. In preparation for the Rite of Final Commitment, the oblate candidate will spend some time in recollection. This process will be determined by the monastery of the candidate's choice and can take the form of: (1) a weekend retreat at the monastery during the last six months leading up to the candidate's Final Commitment, (2) attendance at one of the monastic community retreats, and/or (3) being present at a one-day retreat at the candidate's chosen monastery (or wherever the oblate office has scheduled it) immediately prior to the final commitment day.

Rite of Final Commitment. The oblate candidate will probably make her or his Final Commitment at Eucharist on the day mutually determined by the candidate and chosen monastery (often on a type of oblate renewal day, but there are exceptions). At that time the new oblate will receive a symbol of the director of oblates or the monastery's choice (e.g., an oblate pin, Benedictine medal, or the like). The monastery will retain the document of Final Commitment signed by the oblate but could also give the oblate a type of certificate of oblation.

Period of support and prayer for the new oblate. During the year following her or his Final Commitment, the new oblate will be supported in prayer by the monastic community and the community of oblates.

Ongoing Formation

All of us Christians recognize the need for continuous help along the way of our spiritual journey. For every step we take forward in the spiritual life we may take two backward. With Saint Paul we can say: "For I do not do what I want, but I do the very thing I hate" (Rom 7:15). Since oblates commit themselves to ongoing conversion according to Benedictine and Gospel values, it is important that they continue practices and behaviors that aid their efforts. The following are key elements in ongoing formation:

1. Praying at least one Liturgy of the Hours daily;
2. Reading Scripture daily and meditating on it and its life application as in *lectio divina;*
3. Attending oblate special days at the monastery, oblate discussion groups, meetings, and Oblate Renewal Day if the monastery has one;
4. Attending an annual retreat;
5. Participating in church and civic community groups and in activities that promote Christian values such as the value of reverence for life, justice, equality, peace, ecumenism, and morality in the workplace and society; in addition, performing spiritual and corporal works of mercy.

Church Regulations for Oblates

To avoid any confusion or misunderstandings about the oblate vocation as related to the monastic vowed life, efforts toward clarification have resulted in such statements as the following:

1. "Though Oblates belong to specific Benedictine communities juridically they are not considered members of the monastic order. . . . Oblates are associated with monastic communities in a bond of prayer, love and commitment only."[1]
2. In church law, Oblates of Saint Benedict are considered "a private association of the faithful."[2]
3. Oblate life is distinct from various other groups in the church, such as Marriage Encounter, Cursillo, etc., and is a true vocation of the church.[3]

Transfer of Oblation

For geographical or other carefully considered reasons, an oblate of a monastery may decide to transfer his or her affiliation to a different monastic community. In such a case the oblate notifies the director of oblates of the monastery with which she or he is affiliated and also issues a request to the director of oblates of the other monastery.

Example. Should an oblate from another monastery desire to transfer affiliation to Saint Benedict's Monastery in Saint Joseph, Minnesota, she or he should seek permission from the director of oblates of the original monastery of affiliation. The oblate should then convey to the director of oblates at Saint Benedict's Monastery the following: (1) a copy of the letter for permission to transfer, signed by the director of oblates of the original monastery of affiliation and (2) a copy of his or her certificate of oblation.

Guidelines for Oblates of Saint Benedict[4]

In accord with the values of Benedictine spirituality and the spirit of Vatican II regarding the laity, many oblate directors at various monasteries have endorsed the following guidelines for oblates:

1. "Oblates strive to be loyal and active members of Christ and the Church." Nourished by the sacraments, they witness to Christ, promote the salvation of humankind, foster the ecumenical spirit, and spread the Word of God as they serve others.

2. "Oblates strive for their own continued Christian renewal and improvement." They make the study and reading of Scripture an important part of their lives and try to improve spiritually, intellectually, socially, and culturally as their state in life permits.

3. "Oblates strive to be men and women of practical spirituality." They try to live and work with an awareness of God's ever presence, trust in God through their daily crosses and burdens, are concerned about the needs of others, and use God's gifts prudently.

4. "Oblates strive to be men and women of prayer." They take an active and intelligent part in the Mass, try to pray some part of the Divine Office or Liturgy of the Hours daily as their life

situations permit, and are mindful of the liturgical seasons of the church year to which they blend their public and private prayer.

5. "Oblates strive to be men and women of Christian virtue." They believe, hope, and trust in God and try to love God and others in thought, word, and deed. They foster a deep respect for the God-given rights of others, especially for human life itself and for freedom of religion. They practice prudence, justice, and charity in the concrete situations of their daily lives, and try to be good stewards of their God-given gifts, balancing all in moderation.

6. "Oblates foster a spirit of community" by keeping in touch with their monastic community, visiting it occasionally and supporting its works. They foster the spirit of community in their own families and in the groups/organizations to which they belong.

7. "Oblates are men and women of peace." They use rightful means to establish peace around them and in the world.

CHAPTER 7

Reading List

The following lists of books are but a meager offering in light of the many excellent works that have been written, are in the process of being written, and will be produced in the future. While the books are listed under specific headings, some books in one group could qualify for placement in another, and vice versa. In addition *know that there is no claim whatsoever that the books chosen are the very best for each category or for each individual seeker of God.* Please view the lists as a *beginning* only, a mere suggested path that offers some choices, and which may lead you toward other helpful works on your spiritual journey. If even only one of these books motivates you and enriches your spiritual life, the mission of the lists will have been accomplished.

Books on the Rule of Benedict and Benedictine Values

Barry, Patrick. *Saint Benedict's Rule.* York, UK: Ampleforth Abbey Press, 1997.

Barry, Patrick, Richard Yeo, Kathleen Norris, et al. *Wisdom from the Monastery: The Rule of Benedict for Everyday Life.* Collegeville, MN: Liturgical Press, 2006.

Baudoz, Jean-François. *With Christ: The Gospel under the Guidance of Saint Benedict.* Translated by *Madeleine M. Beaumont.* Collegeville, MN: Liturgical Press, 2005.

Benedictine Daily Prayer: A Short Breviary. Compiled and edited by Maxwell E. Johnson. Collegeville, MN: Liturgical Press, 2005.

Benson, Robert. *A Good Neighbor: Benedict's Guide to Community.* Brewster, MA: Paraclete Press, 2009.

Böckmann, Aquinata. *Around the Monastic Table: Growing in Mutual Service and Love.* Collegeville, MN: Liturgical Press, 2009.

———. *Perspectives on the Rule of St. Benedict: Expanding Our Hearts in Christ.* Translated by Matilda Handl and Marianne Burkhard. Edited by Marianne Burkhard. Collegeville, MN: Liturgical Press, 2005.

Bonomo, Carol. *The Abbey up the Hill: A Year in the Life of a Monastic Day-Tripper.* Harrisburg, PA: Morehouse Publishing, 2002.

———. *Humble Pie: St. Benedict's Ladder of Humility.* Harrisburg, PA: Morehouse Publishing, 2003.

Butcher, Carmen Acevedo. *A Life of St. Benedict: Man of Blessing.* Brewster, MA: Paraclete Press, 2006.

Canham, Elizabeth J. *Heart Whispers: Benedictine Wisdom for Today.* Nashville, TN: Upper Room Books, 1999.

Cary-Elwas, Columba. *Work and Prayer: The Rule of St. Benedict for Lay People.* Translated by Catherine Wybourne. Kent, UK: Burns and Oates, 1992.

Casey, Michael. *Fully Human, Fully Divine: An Interactive Christology.* Liguori, MO: Liguori/Triumph, 2004.

———. *A Guide to Living in the Truth: St. Benedict's Teaching on Humility.* Liguori, MO: Liguori/Triumph, 2001.

———. *The Road to Eternal Life: Reflections on the Prologue of Benedict's Rule.* Collegeville, MN: Liturgical Press, 2011.

———. *Sacred Reading: The Ancient Art of Lectio Divina.* Liguori, MO: Triumph Books, 1996.

———. *Strangers to the City: Reflections on the Beliefs and Values of the Rule of St. Benedict.* Brewster, MA: Paraclete Press, 2005.

———. *Towards God: The Western Tradition of Contemplation.* Melbourne: Collins Dove, 1989.

———. *The Undivided Heart.* Petersham, MA: Saint Bede's Publications, 1994.

———. *An Unexciting Life: Reflections on Benedictine Spirituality.* Petersham, MA: Saint Bede's Publications, 2005.

Chittister, Joan. *The Monastery of the Heart: An Invitation to a Meaningful Life.* Katonah, NY: BlueBridge / United Tribes Media, 2011.

———. *The Radical Christian Life: A Year with Saint Benedict.* Collegeville, MN: Liturgical Press, 2011.

———. *The Rule of Benedict: Insights for the Ages.* New York: Crossroad, 1992.

———. *The Rule of Benedict: A Spirituality for the 21st Century.* Chestnut Ridge, NY: Crossroad, 2010.

———. *Twelve Steps to Inner Freedom: Humility Revisited.* Erie, PA: Benetvision, 2003.

———. *Wisdom Distilled from the Daily.* New York: Harper & Row, 1990.

Collins, Gregory. *The Glenstal Book of Icons: Praying with the Glenstal Icons.* Collegeville, MN: Liturgical Press, 2002.

Derkse, Wil. *The Rule of Benedict for Beginners: Spirituality for Daily Life.* Collegeville, MN: Liturgical Press, 2003.

De Vogüé, Adalbert. *Reading Saint Benedict: Reflections on the Rule.* Translated by Colette Friedlander. Kalamazoo, MI: Cistercian Publications, 1994.

———. *The Rule of St. Benedict: A Doctrinal and Spiritual Commentary.* Kalamazoo, MI: Cistercian Publications, 1984.

De Waal, Esther. *A Life-Giving Way: A Commentary on the Rule of St. Benedict.* Collegeville, MN: Liturgical Press, 1995.

———. *Living with Contradiction: Reflections on the Rule of St. Benedict.* Harrisburg, PA: Morehouse Publishing, 1997.

———. *Lost in Wonder: Rediscovering the Spiritual Art of Mindfulness.* Collegeville, MN: Liturgical Press, 2003.

———. *Seeking God: The Way of St. Benedict.* Collegeville, MN: Liturgical Press, 1984. Second edition, 2001.

———. *Seeking Life: The Baptismal Invitation of the Rule of St. Benedict.* Collegeville, MN: Liturgical Press, 2009.

Dean, Eric. *Saint Benedict for the Laity.* Collegeville, MN: Liturgical Press, 1989.

Driscoll, Jeremy. *A Monk's Alphabet: Accidental Reflections of a Monastic in the World.* New York: Random House, 2006.

Dumm, Demetrius. *Cherish Christ above All: The Bible in the Rule of Benedict.* Mahwah, NJ: Paulist Press, 1996.

Earle, Mary C. *Beginning Again: Benedictine Wisdom for Living with Illness.* Harrisburg, PA: Morehouse Publishing, 2004.

Feiss, Hugh. *Essential Monastic Wisdom: Writings on the Contemplative Life.* New York: HarperCollins, 1999.

Foster, David. *Reading with God: Lectio Divina.* New York: Continuum, 2005.

Galbraith, Craig S., and Oliver Galbraith III. *The Benedictine Rule of Leadership: Classic Management Secrets You Can Use Today.* Avon, MA: Adams Media, 2004.

The Glenstal Book of Daily Prayer: A Benedictine Prayer Book. Collegeville, MN: Liturgical Press, 2009.

Gregory the Great. *Life and Miracles of St. Benedict* or *The Second Book of Dialogues.* Translated by Odo J. Zimmermann and Benedict R. Avery. Collegeville, MN: Liturgical Press, 1949. (Text also found on websites.)

Grün, Anselm. *Benedict of Nursia: His Message for Today.* Translated by Linda M. Maloney. Collegeville, MN: Liturgical Press, 2006.

————. *Celibacy—A Fullness of Life*. Translated by Gregory J. Roettger and Luise R. Pugh. Schuyler, NE: BMH Publications, 1993.

————. *The Challenge of Silence*. Translated by Gregory J. Roettger. Schuyler, NE: BMH Publications, 1993.

————. *Prayer and Self-Knowledge*. Translated by Sister M. Frances de Sales Market. Schuyler, NE: BMH Publications, 1993.

Grün, Anselm, and Meinrad Dufner. *Health as a Spiritual Task*. Translated by Gregory J. Roettger. Schuyler, Nebraska: BMH Publications, 1993.

Guenther, Margaret. *At Home in the World: A Rule of Life for the Rest of Us*. New York: Seabury Books, 2006.

————. *My Soul in Silence Waits*. Boston, MA: Cowley Publications, 2000.

Hall, Thelma. *Too Deep for Words: Rediscovering Lectio Divina*. Mahwah, NJ: Paulist Press, 1988.

Henry, Patrick, ed. *Benedict's Dharma*. New York: Riverhead Books, 2001.

Holdaway, Gervase, ed. *The Oblate Life*. Collegeville, MN: Liturgical Press, 2008.

Holtz, Albert. *Walking in Valleys of Darkness: A Benedictine Journey through Troubled Times*. Harrisburg, PA: Morehouse Publishing, 2011.

Howard, Katherine. *Praying with Benedict*. Winona, MN: St. Mary's Press, 1996.

Hume, Cardinal Basil. *In Praise of Benedict: 480–1980 A.D.* Petersham, MA: Saint Bede's Publications, 1981.

————. *Searching for God*. Mahwah, NJ: Paulist Press, 1977.

Jamison, Christopher. *Finding Sanctuary: Monastic Steps for Everyday Life*. Collegeville, MN: Liturgical Press, 2006.

Kardong, Terrence G. *Asking Benedict: A Study Program on the Rule of St. Benedict for Classes and Private Use*. Richardton, ND: Assumption Abbey Press, 1992.

————. *Benedict's Rule: A Translation and Commentary*. Collegeville, MN: Liturgical Press, 1996.

————. *The Benedictines*. Collegeville, MN: Liturgical Press, 1988.

————. *Conversation with St. Benedict: The Rule in Today's World*. Collegeville, MN: Liturgical Press, 2012.

————. *Day by Day with Saint Benedict*. Collegeville, MN: Liturgical Press, 2005.

————. *Pillars of Community: Four Rules of Pre-Benedictine Monastic Life*. Collegeville, MN: Liturgical Press, 2010.

————, trans. *The Life of St. Benedict by Gregory the Great*. Collegeville, MN: Liturgical Press, 2009.

Kline, Francis. *Lovers of the Place: Monasticism Loose in the Church.* Kalamazoo, MI: Cistercian Publications, 1997.

Kodell, Jerome. *Don't Trust the Abbot: Musings from the Monastery.* Collegeville, MN: Liturgical Press, 2009.

Longenecker, Dwight. *Listen, My Son: St. Benedict for Fathers.* Harrisburg, PA: Morehouse Publishing, 1999.

———. *St. Benedict and St. Thérèse: The Little Rule & the Little Way.* Huntington, IN: Our Sunday Visitor, 2002.

Magrassi, Archbishop Mariano. *Praying the Bible: An Introduction to Lectio Divina.* Translated by Edward Hagman. Collegeville, MN: Liturgical Press, 1998.

Marett-Crosby, Anthony, ed. *The Benedictine Handbook.* Collegeville, MN: Liturgical Press, 2003.

Masini, Mario. *Lectio Divina: An Ancient Prayer That Is Ever New.* Translated by Edmund C. Lane. New York: Alba House, 1998.

McCabe, Maureen. *Inside the Psalms: Reflections for Novices.* Kalamazoo, MI: Cistercian Publications, 2005.

McQuistin II, John. *Always We Begin Again: The Benedictine Way of Living.* Harrisburg, PA: Morehouse Publishing, 2011.

Merrill, Nan C. *Psalms for Praying.* New York: Continuum, 1999.

Merton, Thomas. *A Book of Hours.* Edited by Kathleen Deignan. Notre Dame, IN: Ave Maria Press, 2007.

Mundy, Linus. *A Retreat with Benedict and Bernard: Seeking God Alone—Together.* Cincinnati, OH: Saint Anthony Messenger Press, 1998.

Norris, Kathleen. *The Cloister Walk.* New York: Riverhead, 1996.

Oury, Guy-Marie. *A Monastic Pilgrimage: Following in the Steps of St. Benedict.* Petersham, MA: Saint Bede's Publications, 1998.

Pennington, M. Basil. *Lectio Divina: Renewing the Ancient Practice of Praying the Scriptures.* New York: Crossroad, 1998.

———. *Light from the Cloister.* Mahwah, NJ: Paulist Press, 1991.

———. *Listen with Your Heart: Spiritual Living with the Rule of St. Benedict.* Brewster, MA: Paraclete Press, 2007.

Pratt, Lonni Collins, and Daniel Homan. *Benedict's Way: An Ancient Monk's Insights for a Balanced Life.* Chicago: Loyola Press, 2000.

———. *Radical Hospitality: Benedict's Way of Love.* New expanded ed. Brewster, MA: Paraclete Press, 2011.

Rippinger, Joel. *The Benedictine Order in the United States: An Interpretive History.* Collegeville, MN: Liturgical Press, 1990.

Robinson, David. *Ancient Paths: Discover Christian Formation the Benedictine Way.* Brewster, MA: Paraclete Press, 2010.

————. *The Christian Family Toolbox: 52 Benedictine Activities for the Home.* New York: Crossroad, 2001.

————. *The Family Cloister: Benedictine Wisdom for the Home.* New York: Crossroad, 2000.

Rule of Saint Benedict 1980. Edited by Timothy Fry. Collegeville, MN: Liturgical Press, 1981.

Rupert, Fidelis, and Anselm Grün. *Christ in the Brother: According to the Rule of St. Benedict and in Everyday Life.* Translated by Gregory J. Roettger. Schuyler, NE: BMH Publications, 1992.

Simon, G. A., ed. *Commentary for Benedictine Oblates.* Translated by Leonard J. Doyle. Eugene, OR: Wipf and Stock Publisher, 2009.

Smith, Cyprian. *The Path of Life.* York, UK: Ampleforth Abbey Press, 1995. Reprinted 1996.

Srubas, Rachel M. *Oblation: Meditations on St. Benedict's Rule.* Brewster, MA: Paraclete Press, 2006.

Stewart, Columba. *Prayer and Community.* Maryknoll, NY: Orbis Books, 1998.

Sutera, Judith, ed. *Work of God: Benedictine Prayer.* Collegeville, MN: Liturgical Press, 1997.

Swan, Laura, ed. *The Benedictine Tradition: Spirituality in History.* Collegeville, MN: Liturgical Press, 2007.

————. *Engaging Benedict: What the Rule Can Teach Us Today.* Notre Dame, IN: Ave Maria Press, 2005.

Talbot, John Michael. *Blessings of St. Benedict.* Collegeville, MN: Liturgical Press, 2011.

Taylor, Brian C. *Spirituality for Everyday Living: An Adaptation of the Rule of St. Benedict.* Collegeville, MN: Liturgical Press, 1989.

Tinsley, Ambrose. *Carried by the Current: A Benedictine Perspective.* Dublin: Columba Press, 2004.

————. *Pax: The Benedictine Way.* Dublin: Columba Press, 1994.

Tomaine, Jane. *St. Benedict's Toolbox: The Nuts and Bolts of Everyday Benedictine Living.* Harrisburg, PA: Morehouse Publishing, 2005.

Tvedten, Benet. *A Share in the Kingdom: A Commentary on the Rule of Benedict for Oblates.* Collegeville, MN: Liturgical Press, 1989.

Vermeiren, Korneel. *Praying with Benedict: Prayer in the Rule of St. Benedict.* Translated by Richard Yeo. Kalamazoo, MI: Cistercian Publications, 1999.

Vest, Norvene. *Desiring Life: Benedict on Wisdom and the Good Life.* Cambridge, MA: Cowley Publications, 2006.

———. *Friend of the Soul: A Benedictine Spirituality of Work.* Boston: Cowley Publications, 1997.

———. *Gathered in the Word: Praying the Scriptures in Small Groups.* Nashville, TN: Upper Room Books, 1996.

———. *No Moment Too Small: Rhythms of Silence, Prayer and Holy Reading.* Boston: Cowley Publications, 1994.

———. *Preferring Christ: A Devotional Commentary & Workbook on the Rule of Saint Benedict.* Trabuco Canyon, CA: Source Books, 1991. Reprinted Harrisburg, PA: Morehouse Publishing, 2004.

Ware, Corinne. *Saint Benedict on the Freeway: A Rule of Life for the 21st Century.* Nashville, TN: Abingdon Press, 2001.

Wiederkehr, Macrina. *The Song of the Seed: A Monastic Way of Tending the Soul.* San Francisco: HarperCollins, 1995.

———. *A Tree Full of Angels: Seeing the Holy in the Ordinary.* San Francisco: Harper and Row, 1988.

Wilkes, Paul. *Beyond the Walls: Monastic Wisdom for Everyday Living.* New York: Image / Doubleday, 1999. Second edition, 2000.

General Books for Spiritual Growth

Aigner, Jill. *Foundations Last Forever: Lectio Divina, A Mode of Scripture Prayer.* Mount Angel, OR: Priory Productions, 1987.

Beckwith, Michael Bernard. *Spiritual Liberation: Fulfilling Your Soul's Potential.* New York: Atria Books, 2008.

Bede Griffiths: Essential Writings. Modern Spiritual Masters Series. Maryknoll, NY: Orbis Books, 2004.

Bianchi, Enzo. *Praying the Word.* Kalamazoo, MI: Cistercian Publications, 1998.

Bondi, Robert C. *In Ordinary Time: Healing the Wounds of the Heart.* Nashville, TN: Abingdon Press, 2001.

Bonhoeffer, Dietrich. *The Cost of Discipleship.* 1st ed. New York: Touchstone, 1995.

Boulding, Maria. *The Coming of God.* 3rd ed. Conception, MO: The Printery House, 2000.

———. *Gateway to Hope: An Exploration of Failure.* Petersham, MA: Saint Bede's Publications, 1985.

———. *Marked for Life: Prayer in the Easter Christ.* New ed. London: Society for Promoting Christian Knowledge, 1995.

Chapman, John. *Spiritual Letters.* New York: Continuum International Publishing Group, 2003.

Chittister, Joan. *The Breath of the Soul: Reflections on Prayer.* New London, CT: Twenty-Third Publications, 2009.

———. *Welcome to the Wisdom of the World and Its Meaning for You.* Grand Rapids, MI: William B. Eerdmans, 2007.

Cook, Joan E. *Hear, O Heavens and Listen, O Earth: Introduction to the Prophets.* Collegeville, MN: Liturgical Press / Michael Glazier, 2006.

Craghan, John F. *Psalms for All Seasons.* Collegeville, MN: Liturgical Press, 1993.

Cummings, Charles. *The Mystery of the Ordinary.* San Francisco: Harper & Row, 1982.

D'Arcy, Paula. *Waking Up to This Day: Seeing the Beauty Right before Us.* Maryknoll, NY: Orbis Books, 2009.

D'Elbée, Fr. Jean C. J. *I Believe in Love.* Manchester, NH: Sophia Institute Press, 2001.

Dumm, Demetrius. *Flowers in the Desert: A Spirituality of the Bible.* New York: Paulist Press, 1987. Latrobe, PA: Saint Vincent Archabbey Publications, 2001, repr.

———. *A Mystical Portrait of Jesus: New Perspectives on John's Gospel.* Collegeville, MN: Liturgical Press, 2001.

———. *Praying the Scriptures.* Collegeville, MN: Liturgical Press, 2003.

———. *So We Do Not Lose Heart.* Latrobe, PA: Saint Vincent Archabbey Publications, 2006.

Earle, Mary C. *Broken Body, Healing Spirit: Lectio Divina and Living with Illness.* Harrisburg, PA: Morehouse Publishing, 2003.

Ellsberg, Robert, ed. *Modern Spiritual Masters: Writings on Contemplation and Compassion.* Maryknoll, NY: Orbis Books, 2008.

Funk, Sister Mary Margaret. *Humility Matters for Practicing the Spiritual Life.* New York: Continuum International Publishing Group, 2005.

———. *Thoughts Matter: The Practice of the Spiritual Life.* New York: Continuum, 1998.

———. *Tools Matter for Practicing the Spiritual Life.* New York: Continuum International Publishing Group, 2004.

Griffiths, Bede. *Return to the Center.* Springfield, IL: Templegate Publishers, 1982.

Hall, Sister Jeremy. *Silence, Solitude, Simplicity: A Hermit's Love Affair with a Noisy, Crowded, and Complicated World.* Collegeville, MN: Liturgical Press, 2007.

Harrington, Daniel J. *What Are We Hoping For?: New Testament Images.* Collegeville, MN: Liturgical Press, 2006.

Hays, Edward. *Psalms for Zero Gravity: Prayers for Life's Emigrants.* Leavenworth, KA: Forest of Peace Publishing, 1998.

Holtz, Albert. *Street Wisdom: Connecting with God in Everyday Life*. Mystic, CT: Twenty-Third Publications, 2003.

Hume, Cardinal Basil. *The Mystery of the Incarnation*. Brewster, MA: Paraclete Press, 2000.

Keating, Thomas. *The Better Part: Stages of Contemplative Living*. New York: Continuum, 2000.

———. *Centering Prayer in Daily Life and Ministry*. Edited by Gustave Reininger. New York: Continuum, 1998.

———. *The Divine Indwelling*. New York: Lantern Books, 2001.

———. *The Heart of the World: An Introduction to Contemplative Christianity*. Chestnut Ridge, NY: Crossroad Publishing Company, 2008.

———. *Manifesting God*. New York: Lantern Books, 2005.

———. *Open Mind, Open Heart: The Contemplative Dimension of the Gospel*. New York: Continuum, 1997.

Kushner, Harold S. *Overcoming Life's Disappointments*. New York: Alfred A. Knopf, 2006.

Leseur, Elizabeth. *Selected Writings: Classics of Western Spirituality*. Mahwah, NJ: Paulist Press, 2005.

Lewis, C. S. *Mere Christianity*. New York: HarperCollins, 2001.

Main, John. *The Heart of Creation: The Meditative Way*. New York: Crossroad, 1989.

———. *The Way of Unknowing: Expanding Spiritual Horizons through Meditation*. New York: Crossroad, 1990.

May, Gerald. *Simply Sane: The Spirituality of Mental Health*. Chestnut Ridge, NY: Crossroad, 1993.

McDonnell, Thomas P., ed. *A Thomas Merton Reader*. New York: Image / Doubleday, 1996.

McQuiston, John II. *Always We Begin Again: The Benedictine Way of Living*. Harrisburg, PA: Morehouse Publishing, 1996.

Merton, Thomas. *Basic Principles of Monastic Spirituality*. Springfield, IL: Templegate Publishers, 1996.

———. *I Have Seen What I Was Looking For: Selected Spiritual Writings*. Edited by M. Basil Pennington. Hyde Park, NY: New City Press, 2005.

———. *New Seeds of Contemplation*. Revised ed. New York: New Directions, 1974.

———. *Thomas Merton: Essential Writings Selected*. Introduction by Christine M. Bochen. Maryknoll, NY: Orbis Books, 2000.

Metz, Johannes Baptist. *Poverty of Spirit*. Revised ed. Translated by John Drury. Mahwah, NJ: Paulist Press, 1998.

Miller, Robert J. *Falling into Faith: Lectio Divina Series*. Franklin, WI: Sheed and Ward, 2000.

Nouwen, Henri. *Our Second Birth: Christian Reflections on Death and New Life*. Chestnut Ridge, NY: Crossroad Publishing Company, 2006.

Pennington, M. Basil. *Centered Living: The Way of Centering Prayer*. Liguori, MO: Liguori / Triumph, 1999.

———. *An Invitation to Centering Prayer*. Liguori, MO: Ligouri, 2001.

———. *Living in the Question*. New York: Continuum, 1999.

———. *Seeking His Mind: 40 Meetings with Christ*. Brewster, MA: Paraclete Press, 2002.

———. *True Self / False Self: Unmasking the Spirit Within*. New York: Crossroad, 2000.

Pinchbeck, Daniel. *Notes from the Edge Times*. New York: Tarcher / Penguin, 2010.

Plaiss, Mark. *The Inner Room: A Journey into Lay Monasticism*. Cincinnati, OH: Saint Anthony Messenger Press, 2003.

Rahner, Karl. *The Mystical Way in Everyday Life*. Maryknoll, NY: Orbis Books, 2010.

———. *The Need and the Blessing of Prayer*. 3rd revised ed. Collegeville, MN: Liturgical Press, 1997.

Rohr, Richard. *Everything Belongs: The Gift of Contemplative Prayer*. Chestnut Ridge, NY: Crossroad, 1999.

———. *Falling Upward: A Spirituality for the Two Halves of Life*. San Francisco: Jossey-Bass, 2011.

———. *Immortal Diamond: The Search for Our True Self*. San Francisco: Jossey-Bass, 2013.

———. *The Naked Now*. Chestnut Ridge, NY: Crossroad, 2009.

Rolheiser, Ronald. *Against an Infinite Horizon: The Finger of God in Our Everyday Lives*. New York: Crossroad, 1996.

———. *Forgotten Among the Lilies: Learning to Love beyond Our Fear*. New York: Doubleday, 2005.

———. *The Holy Longing: The Search for a Christian Spirituality*. New York: Doubleday, 1999.

———. *Our One Great Act of Fidelity: Waiting for Christ in the Eucharist*. New York: Doubleday, 2011.

———. *The Restless Heart: Finding Our Spiritual Home in Times of Loneliness*. New York: Random House, 2006.

———. *The Shattered Lantern: Rediscovering a Felt Presence of God*. Chestnut Ridge, NY: Crossroad, 2001.

Rooney, Don. *Journeying with the Bible*. Collegeville, MN: Liturgical Press, 2003.

Schmidt, Joseph. *Praying Our Experiences.* Winona, MN: St. Mary's Press, 2000.
Steindl-Rast, David. *Common Sense Spirituality: The Essential Wisdom of David Steindl-Rast.* Chestnut Ridge, NY: Crossroad, 2008.
———. *Words of Common Sense for Mind, Body, and Soul.* Radnor, PA: Templeton Foundation Press, 2002.
Taylor, Barbara Brown. *An Altar in the World: A Geography of Faith.* New York: HarperOne, 2010.
Wiederkehr, Macrina. *The Song of the Seed: A Monastic Way of Tending the Soul.* San Francisco: HarperSanFrancisco, 1995.

Some Sources of Benedictine History

Barry, Patrick. *St. Benedict and Christianity in England.* Leominster, UK: Gracewing / Ampleforth Abbey Press, 1995.
Beattie, Gordon. *Gregory's Angels.* Leominster, UK: Gracewing, 1997.
Brooke, Christopher Nugent Lawrence. *The Age of the Cloister: The Story of Monastic Life in the Middle Ages.* Mahwah, NJ: HiddenSpring / Paulist Press, 2003.
Derrick, Christopher. *The Rule of Peace: St. Benedict and the European Future.* Petersham, MA: Saint Bede's Publications, 1980.
Farmer, David Hugh, ed. *Benedict's Disciples.* 2nd ed. Leominster, UK: Gracewing, 1995.
Girgen, Sister Incarnata. *Behind the Beginnings: Benedictine Women in America.* Saint Paul, MN: North Central Publishing Co., 1981.
Hart, Patrick, ed. *A Monastic Vision for the Twenty-first Century: Where Do We Go from Here?* Kalamazoo, MI: Cistercian Publications, 2006.
Hume, Cardinal Basil. *In Praise of Benedict.* Petersham, MA: Saint Bede's Publications, 2002.
Lawrence, C. H. *Medieval Monasticism: Forms of Religious Life in Western Europe in the Middle Ages.* 3rd ed. New York: Longman, 2000.
McDonald, Sister Grace. *With Lamps Burning.* Saint Paul, MN: North Central Publishing Co., 1980. (The history of St. Benedict's Monastery, St. Joseph, Minnesota.)
Oetgen, Jerome. *An American Abbot: Boniface Wimmer, O.S.B., 1809–1887.* Revised ed. Toronto: Scholarly Book Services, 2002.
Rademacher, Sister Evin, et al. *With Hearts Expanded: Transformation in the Lives of Benedictine Women St. Joseph, Minnesota 1957 to 2000.* St. Cloud, MN: North Star Press, 2000.
Rippinger, Joel. *The Benedictine Order in the United States: An Interpretive History.* Collegeville, MN: Liturgical Press, 1990.

Schmitt, Miriam, and Linda Kulzer, eds. *Medieval Women Monastics: Women's Wellsprings*. Collegeville, MN: Liturgical Press, 1996.

Scott, Geoffrey. *Gothic Rage Undone: English Monks in the Age of Enlightenment*. Bath, UK: Downside Abbey, 1992.

Some Sources about Monasticism and Christianity

Bondi, Roberta C. *To Love as God Loves: Conversations with the Early Church*. Minneapolis: Augsburg Fortress Press, 1987.

Casey, Michael. *Toward God: The Ancient Wisdom of Western Prayer*. Liguori, MO: Triumph Books, 1995. 1st US edition, 1996.

De Dreuille, Mayeul. *From East to West: A History of Monasticism*. New York: Crossroad, 1999.

Egan, Harvey D. *An Anthology of Christian Mysticism*. Collegeville, MN: Liturgical Press / Pueblo Book, 1996.

Johnson, Penelope D. *Equal in Monastic Profession: Religious Women in Medieval France*. Chicago: University of Chicago Press, 1991.

Jones, Robert C. *Monks and Monasteries: A Brief History*. Acworth, GA: self-published, 2010.

King, Peter. *Western Monasticism: A History of the Monastic Movement in the Latin Church*. Kalamazoo, MI: Cistercian Publications, 1999.

Keller, David G. R. *Oasis of Wisdom: The Worlds of the Desert Fathers and Mothers*. Collegeville, MN: Liturgical Press, 2005.

Kline, Francis. *Lovers of the Place: Monasticism Loose in the Church*. Collegeville, MN: Liturgical Press, 1997.

Knowles, David. *Christian Monasticism*. World University Library.

Lawrence, Clifford Hugh. *Medieval Monasticism: Forms of Religious Life in Western Europe in the Middle Ages*. 3rd ed. London: Longman, 2001.

Leclerq, Jean. *The Love of Learning and the Desire for God: A Study of Monastic Culture*. 3rd ed. Translated by Catharine Misrahi. New York: Fordham University Press, 1982.

Lindberg, Carter. *A Brief History of Christianity*. Malden, MA: Blackwell Publications, 2006.

Marett-Crosby, Anthony. *The Foundations of Christian England*. Leominster, UK : Gracewing, 1997.

Markus, R. A. *The End of Ancient Christianity*. Cambridge, UK: Cambridge University Press, 1991.

Merton, Thomas. *Cassian and the Fathers: Initiation into the Monastic Tradition*. Kalamazoo, MI: Cistercian Publications, 2005.

Mullins, Edwin. *Cluny: In Search of God's Lost Empire*. New York: BlueBridge, 2006.

Stewart, Columba. *World of the Desert Fathers*. Kalamazoo, MI: Cistercian Publications, 1986.

Venarde, Bruce L. *Women's Monasticism and Medieval Society: Nunneries in France and England, 890–1215*. Ithaca, NY; London: Cornell University Press, 1997.

Vivian, Tim, ed. *Journeying into God: Seven Early Monastic Rules*. Translated by Tim Vivian. Minneapolis, MN: Fortress Press, 1996.

Ward, Benedicta. *Harlots of the Desert: A Study of Repentance in Early Monastic Sources*. Kalamazoo, MI: Cistercian Publications, 1987.

———. *Wisdom of the Desert Fathers*. Fairacres, Oxford: SLG Press, 1981. Reprinted by Lion Publishing Corporation, Colorado Springs, CO, 2002.

Some Biographical-Type Reading

Boulding, Maria, ed. *A Touch of God: Eight Monastic Journeys*. Petersham, MA: Saint Bede's Publications, 1982.

Charles, William, ed. *Basil Hume—Ten Years On*. London: Burns & Oates, 2009.

Cunningham, Lawrence. *Thomas Merton and the Monastic Vision*. Grand Rapids, MI: William B. Eerdmans, 1999.

Day, Dorothy. *The Long Loneliness: Autobiography*. San Francisco: Harper, 1997.

De Wohl, Louis. *Citadel of God: A Novel about St. Benedict*. Fort Collins, CO: Ignatius Press, 1994. (Though in novel form, it is considered to be historically accurate.)

Griffiths, Bede. *A Human Search: Bede Griffiths Reflects on His Life*. Edited by John Swindells. Liguori, MO: Triumph Books, 1997.

Howard, Anthony. *Basil Hume the Monk Cardinal*. London: Headline Publishing Group, 2006.

John XXIII, Pope. *Journal of a Soul*. Translated by Dorothy White. New York: Signet Books, 1965.

Johns, Laurentia, ed. *Touched by God: Ten Monastic Journeys*. London: Burns & Oates, 2008.

Kulzer, Linda, and Roberta Bondi, eds. *Benedict in the World: Portraits of Monastic Oblates*. Collegeville, MN: Liturgical Press, 2002.

Maddocks, Fiona. *Hildegard of Bingen: The Woman of Her Age*. New York: Doubleday, 2001.

Markus, R. A. *Gregory the Great and His World*. Cambridge, UK: Cambridge University Press, 1997.

Martin, James. *Becoming Who You Are: Insights on the True Self from Thomas Merton and Other Saints*. Mahwah, NJ: HiddenSpring / Paulist Press, 2006.

McGinnis, Mark W. *Wisdom of the Benedictine Elders: Thirty of America's Oldest Monks and Nuns Share Their Lives' Greatest Lessons*. New York: BlueBridge, 2005.

Merton, Thomas. *The Seven Story Mountain*. New York: Harcourt, Brace, Jovanovich, 1978.

Miller, William. *Dorothy Day: A Biography*. San Francisco: Harper & Row, 1982.

Mott, Michael. *The Seven Story Mountains of Thomas Merton*. San Diego: Harcourt, Brace, Jovanovich / Harvest, 1993.

Pennington, M. Basil. *Thomas Merton, My Brother*. Hyde Park, NY: New City Press, 2002.

Richards, Jeffrey. *Consul of God: The Life and Times of Gregory the Great*. Boston: Routledge and Kegan, 1980.

Royal, Robert. *The Catholic Martyrs of the Twentieth Century: A Comprehensive World History*. Chestnut Ridge, NY: Crossroad, 2006.

Shannon, William. *Anselm: The Joy of Faith*. New York: Crossroad, 1999.

Spink, Kathryn. *Mother Teresa: A Complete Authorized Biography*. New York: HarperCollins, 1997.

Stramara, Daniel F. *Driven By the Spirit: The Life of St. Frances of Rome*. Pecos, NM: Dove Publications, 1992.

Surprised By Truth: Eleven Converts Give the Biblical and Historical Reasons for Becoming Catholic. Edited by Patrick Madrid. San Diego: Basilica Press, 1994.

Thérèse of Lisieux, Saint. *Story of a Soul*. Translated by John Clarke. Washington, DC: Institute of Carmelite Studies Publications, 1975.

Tierney, Mark. *Blessed Columba Marmion: A Short Biography*. Collegeville, MN: Liturgical Press, 2001.

Tvedten, Benet. *The Motley Crew*. Collegeville, MN: Liturgical Press, 2007.

———. *The View from a Monastery: The Vowed Life and Its Cast of Many Characters*. Brewster, MA: Paraclete Press, 2006.

Vest, Norvene. *Benedict: Stories of the Great Saint*. Naperville, IL: Source Books, 1997.

Wilkes, Paul, ed. *Merton: By Those Who Knew Him Best*. New York: HarperCollins, 1984.

Miscellaneous and General Sacred Reading

Albom, Mitch. *The Five People You Meet in Heaven*. New York: Hyperion, 2003.

Arinze, Cardinal Francis. *Meeting Other Believers: The Risks and Rewards of Interreligious Dialogue*. Huntington, IN: Our Sunday Visitor, 1998.

Arnold, Johann Christoph. *I Tell You a Mystery: Life, Death, and Eternity.* Farmington, PA: Plough Publishing House, 1996.

Arts, Herwig. *God, the Christian, and Human Suffering.* Translated by Helen Rolfson. Collegeville, MN: Liturgical Press, 1993.

Bamberg, Corona. *The Cost of Being Human.* Translated by Sister Margretta Nathe. Denville, NJ: Dimension Books, 1980.

Bangley, Bernard. *Nearer to the Heart of God.* Brewster, MA: Paraclete Press, 2005.

Barrett, Mark. *Crossings: Reclaiming the Landscape of Our Lives.* Harrisburg, PA: Morehouse Publishing, 2002.

Barry, David. *Smaragdus of St. Michael: Commentary on the Rule of St. Benedict.* Kalamazoo, MI: Cistercian Publications, 2006.

Barry, William A. *Finding God In All Things.* Notre Dame, IN: Ave Maria Press, 1991.

———. *God's Passionate Desire and Our Response.* Notre Dame, IN: Ave Maria Press, 1993.

Benson, Robert. *A Good Life: Benedict's Guide to Everyday Joy.* Brewster, MA: Paraclete Press, 2004.

Bernardin, Cardinal Joseph. *The Gift of Peace.* Chicago: Loyola Press, 1997.

Bosco, Antoinette. *The Pummeled Heart: Finding Peace through Pain.* Mystic, CT: Twenty-Third Publications, 1994.

Chervin, Ronda. *Spiritual Friendship: Darkness and Light.* Boston: Pauline Books and Media, 1992.

Ciorra, Anthony J. *Everyday Mysticism: Cherishing the Holy.* Kalamazoo, MI: Cistercian Publications, 1995.

Cooper, Austin. *Julian of Norwich: Reflections on Selected Texts.* Mystic, CT: Twenty-Third Publications, 1988.

Day, Dorothy. *Wisdom from Dorothy Day: A Radical Love.* Edited by Patricia Mitchell. Ijamsville, MD: The Word Among Us Press, 2000.

The Desert Fathers. Translated by Helen Waddell. Ann Arbor: University of Michigan Press, 1998.

Durka, Gloria. *Praying with Julian of Norwich.* Winona, MN: Saint Mary's Press, 1989.

Egan, Harvey D. *An Anthology of Christian Mysticism.* Collegeville, MN: Liturgical Press, 1991.

Evely, Louis. *Suffering: Reflections on the Mystery of Human Pain and Suffering.* New York: Herder and Herder, 1967. Reprinted by Image Books, 1974.

Gateley, Edwina. *Mothers, Sisters, Daughters: Standing on Their Shoulders.* Maryknoll, NY: Orbis Books, 2012.

Green, Thomas H. *Prayer and Common Sense*. Notre Dame, IN: Ave Maria Press, 1995.

Groeschel, Benedict. *Arise From Darkness: What to Do When Life Doesn't Make Sense*. Fort Collins, CO: Ignatius Press, 1995.

———. *Heaven in Our Hands: Receiving the Blessings We Long For*. Ann Arbor, MI: Servant Publications, 1994.

———. *The Journey toward God: In the Footsteps of the Great Spiritual Writers—Catholic, Protestant, and Orthodox*. With Kevin Perrotta. Ann Arbor, MI: Servant Publications, 2000.

Gustin, Marilyn. *Living the Liturgy: The Mass as Personal Spiritual Growth*. Liguori, MO: Liguori Publications, 1993.

Hahn, Scott, and Kimberly Hahn. *Rome, Sweet Rome—Our Journey to Catholicism*. San Francisco: Ignatius Press, 1993.

Hart, Patrick, and Jonathan Montaldo, eds. *The Intimate Merton: His Life from His Journals*. San Francisco: HarperSanFrancisco, 2001.

Hauser, Richard J. *Finding God in Troubled Times: The Holy Spirit and Suffering*. Chicago: Loyola Press, 2002.

Hays, Edward. *Chasing Joy: Musings on Life in a Bittersweet World*. Notre Dame, IN: Ave Maria Press, 2007.

Helldorfer, Martin C. *The Work Trap: Rediscovering Leisure, Redefining Work*. Mystic, CT: Twenty-Third Publications, 1995.

Hershey, Terry. *Sacred Necessities: Gifts for Living with Passion, Purpose, and Grace*. Notre Dame, IN: Sorin Books, 2005.

Holtz, Albert. *Pilgrim Road: A Benedictine Journey through Lent*. Harrisburg, PA: Morehouse Publishing, 2006.

———. *Street Wisdom: Connecting with God in Everyday Life*. Mystic, CT: Twenty-Third Publications, 2003.

Holyhead, Verna A., and Lynne Muir. *The Gift of St. Benedict*. Victoria, Australia: John Garrett Publishing, 2002.

Howse, Christopher, ed. *The Best Spiritual Reading Ever*. New York: Continuum, 2003.

Huerre, Denis. *Letters to My Brothers and Sisters*. Collegeville, MN: Liturgical Press, 1991.

Johnson, Barbara. *Pain Is Inevitable, but Misery Is Optional: So Stick a Geranium in Your Hat and Be Happy*. Dallas: Word Publishing, 1990, 1993, 2004.

Johnston, William, ed. *The Cloud of Unknowing*. New York: Image / Doubleday Dell Publishing Group, 1973.

Julian of Norwich. *Revelations of Divine Love*. Selected by James Walsh. London: Catholic Truth Society, 1981.

Kim, James W. *Contemplation 2000: St. John of the Cross for Today*. Petersham, MA: Saint Bede's Publications, 1997.

Lewis, C. S. *The Screwtape Letters*. New York: The Macmillan Company, 1961.

Luti, J. Mary. *Teresa of Avila's Way*. Collegeville, MN: Liturgical Press / Michael Glazier Books, 1991.

Martini, Cardinal Carlo. *What Am I That You Care for Me? Praying with the Psalms*. Translated by Dame Mary Groves. Collegeville, MN: Liturgical Press, 1992.

May, Gerald, G. *The Awakened Heart: Opening Yourself to the Love You Need*. New York: HarperCollins, 1991.

McEntyre, Marilyn Chandler. *Caring for Words in a Culture of Lies*. Grand Rapids, MI: William B. Eerdmans Publisher, 2009.

McKenna, Briege. *Miracles Do Happen: God Can Do the Impossible*. New ed. Dublin: Veritas Publications, 1998.

McNamara, William. *Mystical Passion: Spirituality for a Bored Society*. Mahwah, NJ: Paulist Press, 1977.

McNeil, Donald P., Henri J. M. Nouwen, and Douglas Morrison. *Compassion: A Reflection on Christian Life*. New York: Doubleday, 1983.

Meyer, Marvin. *The Gospels of Mary: The Secret Tradition of Mary Magdalene, the Companion of Jesus*. San Francisco: Harper San Francisco, 2004.

Millett, Craig Ballard. *In God's Image: Archetypes of Women in Scripture*. San Diego: LuraMedia, 1991.

Mitch, Marvin L. Krier. *The Challenge and Spirituality of Catholic Social Teaching*. Rev. ed. Maryknoll, NY: Orbis Books, 2011.

Moore, Thomas. *Dark Nights of the Soul: A Guide to Finding Your Way through Life's Ordeals*. New York: Gotham Books, 2004.

———. *The Soul's Religion: Cultivating a Profound Spiritual Way of Life*. New York: Harper Collins, 2002.

Morice, Rev. Henri. *Why Bad Things Happen to Good Catholics*. Manchester, NH: Sophia Institute Press, 2001.

Morrison, Douglas A., and Christopher P. Witt. *From Loneliness to Love*. Mahwah, NJ: Paulist Press, 1989.

Muldoon, Tim, ed. *Catholic Identity and the Laity*. Maryknoll, NY: Orbis Books, 2009.

Murray, Matt. *The Father and the Son: My Father's Journey into the Monastic Life*. New York: HarperCollins, 1999.

Muto, Susan Annette. *John of the Cross for Today: The Ascent*. Notre Dame, IN: Ave Maria Press, 1991.

———. *John of the Cross for Today: The Dark Night*. Notre Dame, IN: Ave Maria Press, 1994.

Nataraja, Kim, ed. *Journey to the Heart: Christian Contemplation through the Centuries: An Illustrated Guide*. Maryknoll, NY: Orbis Books, 2011.

Neuhaus, Rev. Richard John. *Death on a Friday Afternoon: Meditations on the Last Words of Jesus*. New York: Basic Books, 2000.

Norris, Kathleen. *Amazing Grace: A Vocabulary of Faith*. New York: Riverhead Books, 1998.

Nouwen, Henri J. M. *Life of the Beloved: Spiritual Living in a Secular World*. New York: Crossroad, 1992.

———. *Our Greatest Gift: A Meditation on Dying and Caring*. New York: HarperCollins, 1994.

———. *Reaching Out: The Three Movements of the Spiritual Life*. New York: Random House, 1986.

———. *The Way of the Heart: Desert Spirituality and Contemporary Ministry*. New York: Seabury Press, 1981.

O'Connor, Patricia. *In Search of Thérèse*. Collegeville, MN: Liturgical Press / Michael Glazier Books, 1987.

O'Donnell, Angela Alaimo. *The Province of Joy: Praying with Flannery O'Connor*. Brewster, MA: Paraclete Press, 2012.

O'Donohue, John. *Anam Cara: A Book of Celtic Wisdom*. New York: Harper-Collins, 1997.

———. *Beauty: The Invisible Embrace*. New York: HarperCollins, 2004.

———. *To Bless the Space between Us: A Book of Blessings*. New York: Doubleday, 2008.

Pallister, Margaret Ann. *Christ, Our Mother of Mercy: Divine Mercy and Compassion in the Theology of the "Shewings" of Julian of Norwich*. New York: Walter de Gruyter, 1992.

Pelphrey, Brant. *Christ, Our Mother: Julian of Norwich*. Collegeville, MN: Liturgical Press / Michael Glazier Books, 1989.

Pennington, M. Basil. *Who Do You Say I Am: Meditations on Jesus' Questions in the Gospel*. New York: New City Press, 2004.

Pfeil, Margaret R., and Tobias L. Winright, eds. *Violence, Transformation, and the Sacred*. Maryknoll, NY: Orbis Books, 2012.

Rahner, Karl. *Encounters with Silence*. Translated by James M. Demske. South Bend, IN: Saint Augustine's Press, 1999.

———. *On Prayer*. Translated by Bruce W. Gillette. Collegeville, MN: Liturgical Press, 1997.

Reininger, Gustave, ed. *Centering Prayer in Daily Life and Ministry*. New York: Continuum, 1998.

Rohr, Richard. *Simplicity: The Freedom of Letting Go*. New York: Crossroad, 2004.

Rolheiser, Ronald. *Secularity and the Gospel: Being Missionaries to our Children*. Chestnut Ridge, NY: Crossroad, 2006.

Rupp Joyce. *The Circle of Life: The Heart's Journey through the Seasons*. Notre Dame, IN: Sorin Books, 2005.

———. *Praying Our Goodbyes*. Notre Dame, IN: Ave Maria Press, 1988.

Samra, Cal. *The Joyful Christ: The Healing Power of Humor*. San Francisco: Harper & Row, 1986.

Shannon, William H. *Silence on Fire: The Prayer of Awareness*. New York: Crossroad, 1991.

Sheldrake, Philip. *Befriending Our Desires*. Notre Dame, IN: Ave Maria Press, 1994.

Sinetar, Marsha. *Ordinary People as Monks and Mystics: Lifestyle for Self-Discovery*. Mahwah, NJ: Paulist Press, 1986.

Spink, Kathryn. *Mother Teresa: A Complete Authorized Biography*. New York: HarperCollins, 1997.

Talbot, John Michael. *The World Is My Cloister: Living from the Hermit Within*. Maryknoll, NY: Orbis Books, 2010.

Tugwell, Simon. *Ways of Imperfection: An Exploration of Christian Spirituality*. Springfield, IL: Templegate Publishers, 1985.

Van Kaam, Adrian, and Susan Muto. *Aging Gracefully*. Boston: Pauline Books & Media, 1992.

Vanier, Jean. *The Broken Body: Journey to Wholeness*. Mahwah, NJ: Paulist Press, 1988.

Wicks, Robert J. *Touching the Holy: Ordinariness, Self-Esteem, and Friendship*. Notre Dame, IN: Ave Maria Press, 1992.

Wiederkehr, Macrina. *Behold Your Life: A Pilgrimage through Your Memories*. Notre Dame, IN: Ave Maria Press, 2000.

———. *Gold in Your Memories: Sacred Moments, Glimpses of God*. Notre Dame, IN: Ave Maria Press, 1998.

———. *Seasons of Your Heart: A Monastic Way of Tending the Soul*. San Francisco: Harper San Francisco, 1995.

Directives for Oblate Life

You will find some of these statements under the preceding section, "Church Regulations for Oblates." They are repeated here, along with other directives approved by oblate directors representing many different monasteries, because they continue to help clarify the spirit specific to the Benedictine oblate vocation.

Directives

1. "Oblates of St. Benedict are women and men who have formally associated themselves with a Benedictine monastery in order that they may experience a reciprocal relationship with it in prayer and other good works.

2. "Though oblates commit themselves to live in the spirit of the *Rule of St. Benedict* and the directives for oblates of their specific community, their status is not to be confused with that of 'secular orders,' which are canonically structured with a specific rule and with profession according to that rule after regular periods of formation.

3. "Though oblates belong to specific Benedictine communities, juridically they are not considered members of the monastic order. . . . Oblates are associated with monastic communities in a bond of prayer, love and commitment only.

4. "Oblates are associated with one particular community of Benedictine women or men and seek to incorporate Benedictine values into their everyday life. Thus oblates can be seen as extending the spirit of the monastic community into areas where the community cannot reach or be present. Oblate life is distinct from the various other groups within the Church, such as

Marriage Encounter, Cursillo, Charismatic Renewal, etc., and is a true vocation of the Church.

5. "Oblates of most communities make voluntary donations. Oblates have no dues for membership and are not considered a source of financial support to the community.

6. "Indulgences are available to the Oblates of St. Benedict."[1]

Revised Decree on Indulgences for Oblates

"On May 5, 1975, the Sacred Penitentiary issued the following decree in response to a request that the norms of the Apostolic Constitution, *Indulgentiarum Doctrina*, be applied to indulgences available to Oblates of St. Benedict.

"The Sacred Penitentiary, by special and express Apostolic Authority, graciously grants a plenary indulgence, to be gained by the Oblates of St. Benedict, provided that fulfilling the usual conditions (i.e., confession, communion, and prayer for the intentions of the Holy Father), they pronounce or renew, at least privately, the promise of faithfully observing the statutes of their way of life:

1. "On the days of enrollment and oblation;

2. "On the feast days of: St. Benedict (March 21 or July 11), Sts. Maurus and Placid (January 15), St. Scholastica (February 10), St. Frances of Rome (March 9), and on two additional feast days to be designated by the superior [of the monastery or convent as the case may be, for the oblates affiliated with that community. **Note:** This is to be done once and should be related in some way to feasts celebrated by the community: e.g., the community patronal feast, etc.];

3. "On the 25th and 50th anniversaries of the first oblation.

"These are to be in force *in perpetuum* without the dispatching of an apostolic brief. Anything to the contrary notwithstanding."[2]

Ongoing Formation

As normal, daily life continues for the oblate candidate, the fervor and commitment of early candidacy and oblate finalization times will probably decrease. This is when Benedict's "conversion of morals" or "continuous conversion" may be one of the key factors in a person's life. Change is a given in each human life. As Christians, as Catholics, as Benedictines, we are in transit, on a spiritual journey during which we seek to become ever more like Christ. Because we are human we have to keep deciding, and choosing, and rechoosing those paths that will lead us closer to God. The following suggestions are meant to help us toward the personal transformation that we sought when we took our first step into the Benedictine spirituality we espoused. They should help us on our road to "seeking God" and allow us to stay connected with the essentials.

1. Pray at least one of the Liturgy of the Hours daily.

2. Read the Bible frequently (daily would be ideal) and use it for *lectio divina*.

3. Read part of the Rule daily and use it for *lectio divina*.

4. Make a retreat yearly.

5. Attend the oblate meeting in your area and be involved in the reading and the discussion of the specific chosen books.

6. Read spiritual books, inspiring biographies, online meditations, and similar spiritual aids regularly.

7. Come to your monastery for special days and keep connected to it through various communication channels.

8. Come to your monastery for the annual Oblate Renewal Day if there is one.

9. Attend Eucharist as frequently as possible.

10. Attend workshops on spirituality, theology, Sacred Scripture, and related topics.

11. Talk to God frequently in personal, informal, and uncomplicated prayer.

12. Give of your time and energy in service to others as your schedule and health allow.

13. Stay open to God and recognize the Divine in the ordinary, daily experiences and people in your life.

Prayers

The following examples of prayers similar to the Benedictine Liturgy of the Hours are given in outline form. Please use your Bible to access the psalms and canticles listed.

Morning Prayer

Call to Worship: O Lord, open my lips, and my mouth will proclaim your praise. Glory be to the Father and to the Son and to the Holy Spirit, as it was in the beginning, is now, and ever shall be, world without end. Amen. (Alleluia!)

Hymn

Antiphon (Example): May your love be upon us, O Lord, as we place all our hope in you.

Psalm 63

Canticle: Ezekiel 36:24-28

Psalm 84

Short Reading (From Scripture)

Benedictus Antiphon: Lord, be my rock of safety.

Canticle of Zechariah (Benedictus)

Blessed be the Lord God of Israel,
for he has looked favorably on his people and redeemed them.
He has raised up a mighty savior for us
in the house of his servant David,
as he spoke through the mouth of his holy prophets from of old,
that we would be saved from our enemies and from the hand
of all who hate us.

133

Thus he has shown the mercy promised to our ancestors,
and has remembered his holy covenant,
the oath that he swore to our ancestor Abraham,
to grant us that we, being rescued from the hands of our enemies,
might serve him without fear, in holiness and righteousness
before him all our days.
And you, child, will be called the prophet of the Most High;
for you will go before the Lord to prepare his ways,
to give knowledge of salvation to his people
by the forgiveness of their sins.
By the tender mercy of our God,
the dawn from on high will break upon us,
to give light to those who sit in darkness and in the shadow of
    death,
to guide our feet into the way of peace. (Luke 1:68-79; NRSV)

Benedictus Antiphon: Lord, be my rock of safety.

Our Father

Prayer: Merciful God, help us to live the Gospel of Christ
every day of our lives. Help us to embrace the truth
daily, and to be faithful in our search for you. May
we be a light to all in a world that often seems full
of darkness. We ask this in the name of Jesus, your
Son, who lives forever and ever. Amen.

Closing: May Christ dwell in our hearts through faith.
May charity be the root and foundation of our lives.

Morning Prayer (alternate)

Call to Worship: O Lord, open my lips, and my mouth will proclaim your praise. Glory be to the Father and
to the Son and to the Holy Spirit, as it was in
the beginning, is now, and ever shall be, world
without end. Amen. (Alleluia!)

Hymn

Antiphon: The heavens proclaim God's eternal glory.

Psalm 8

Psalm 90 (Alternate Psalm)

Canticle: 1 Chronicles 29:10b-13

Canticle: Isaiah 40:10-17(Alternate canticle)

Psalm 19

Psalm 57 (Alternate Psalm)

Short Reading

Benedictus Antiphon: A broken and humble heart, O God, you will not scorn.

Canticle of Zechariah (Benedictus as given above)
(Repeat antiphon)

Our Father

Prayer: Loving God, you are with us each day of our lives, supporting us, healing us, blessing us. Protect us from all harm today and always, and guide us toward all that is good. With your unfailing help we can do all things and overcome all obstacles. Thank you for your saving love. We ask this in the name of Jesus, your Son, in union with the Holy Spirit. Amen

Closing: May Christ dwell in our hearts through faith. May charity be the root and foundation of our lives.

Evening Prayer

Call to Worship: O God, come to my assistance. O Lord, make haste to help me. Glory be to the Father and to the Son, and to the Holy Spirit; as it was in the beginning, is now, and ever shall be, world without end. Amen. (Alleluia!)

Hymn

Antiphon (Example):   The greatest among you will be the one who serves the rest.

Psalm 27

Psalm 121

Canticle: 1 Corinthians 12:31b, 13:1-10, 12-13

Reading

Magnificat Antiphon: Lord, I thank you for your faithfulness and love.

> My soul magnifies the Lord,
> and my spirit rejoices in God my Savior,
> for he has looked with favor on the lowliness of his servant.
> Surely, from now on all generations will call me blessed;
> for the Mighty One has done great things for me,
> and holy is his name.
> His mercy is for those who fear him
> from generation to generation.
> He has shown strength with his arm;
> he has scattered the proud in the thoughts of their hearts.
> He has brought down the powerful from their thrones,
> and lifted up the lowly;
> he has filled the hungry with good things,
> and sent the rich away empty.
> He has helped his servant Israel,
> in remembrance of his mercy,
> according to the promise he made to our ancestors,
> to Abraham and to his descendants forever.
>   (Luke 1:46-55; NRSV)

(Repeat antiphon)

Intercessions

Our Father

Prayer: Gracious God, we seek to do your will. It is not
                     easy, and without your constant help, we cannot
                     succeed. Be with us today and always. We put
                     our lives in your hands and trust in your love. We
                     ask this through Jesus Christ, your Son. Amen.

Closing: May the Lord bless and keep us.
                     May Christ dwell in our hearts through faith.

Note: Please consult your Bible for the Psalms and Canticles.

Evening Prayer (alternate)

Psalm 139

Psalm 116

Psalm 86 (Alternate)

Psalm 92 (Alternate)

Canticle: Romans 8:31-35, 37-39

Canticle: Romans 11:33-36 (Alternate)

Canticle: 1 Peter 1:3-9 (Alternate)

Reading

Magnificat Antiphon: Where two or three are gathered in My Name, there I am in the midst of them, says the Lord.

Magnificat (Canticle of Mary)

(Repeat antiphon)

Intercessions

Our Father

Prayer: Wondrous God, full of beauty and goodness, show us how best to serve you. We thank you for all the gifts and talents you have given us. Help us to use them to enrich humankind. May we be a blessing to all we meet. We ask this through Christ our Lord. Amen.

Blessing

Compline (Night Prayer)

Blessing: May Almighty God grant us a peaceful night and a perfect end. Amen.

Leader: Keep alert and watch because your adversary the devil, as a roaring lion goes about seeking to devour. Resist evil, strong in faith. But you, O Lord, have mercy on us.

All: Thanks be to God!

O God, come to my assistance. O Lord, make haste to help me. Glory be to the Father and to the Son, and to the Holy Spirit; as it was in the beginning is now and ever shall be, world without end. Amen. (Alleluia!)

Psalm 91

You who live in the shelter of the Most High,
who abide in the shadow of the Almighty,
will say to the LORD, "My refuge and my fortress;
my God, in whom I trust."

For he will deliver you from the snare of the fowler
and from the deadly pestilence;
he will cover you with his pinions,
and under his wings you will find refuge;
his faithfulness is a shield and buckler.

You will not fear the terror of the night,
or the arrow that flies by day,
or the pestilence that stalks in darkness,
or the destruction that wastes at noonday.

A thousand may fall at your side,
ten thousand at your right hand,
but it will not come near you.

You will only look with your eyes
and see the punishment of the wicked.

Because you have made the LORD your refuge,
the Most High your dwelling place,
no evil shall befall you,
no scourge come near your tent.

For he will command his angels concerning you
to guard you in all your ways.
On their hands they will bear you up,
so that you will not dash your foot against a stone.
You will tread on the lion and the adder,
the young lion and the serpent you will trample under foot.

Those who love me, I will deliver;
I will protect those who know my name.

When they call to me, I will answer them;
I will be with them in trouble,
I will rescue them and honor them.
With long life I will satisfy them,
and show them my salvation.

Psalm 134

Come, bless the LORD, all you servants of the LORD,
who stand by night in the house of the LORD!
Lift up your hands to the holy place,
and bless the LORD.

May the LORD, maker of heaven and earth,
bless you from Zion.

Leader: You, O Lord, are among us and your holy name is called
upon by us. Forsake us not, O Lord our God.
All: Thanks be to God.
Leader: Keep us, O Lord, as the apple of your eye.
All: Protect us under the shadow of your wings.
Leader: Lord, have mercy
All: Christ, have mercy. Lord, have mercy.

Our Father

Prayer: Loving God, visit this home and family. Bless us with your
gracious love and protect us now and always. Renew us with
a restful and peaceful night and send us your blessings. We
pray this in the name of Jesus, your Son and our Savior.
Amen.
Blessing: May the Almighty and merciful God, Father, Son, and Holy
Spirit, bless and keep us. Amen.

Lectio Divina Guide

Choose an event you have lived this day, or any life event that you want to focus on with God.

1. Sit comfortably and in silence in a quiet place of your choosing. Close your eyes and invite God to be with you.

2. When you are ready, recall the event of your life that you want to bring to God. Ponder it; look at it closely to see its potential for a God-message.

3. Check out all aspects of that event in order to find God more directly in it. Where was God in it at the time? Do I find a different aspect of the God-presence in it now? What was God saying to me then? What is God saying to me now?

4. Talk to God about it. Did God let you experience the event to help you to see a way to transform your life? Dialogue with God in prayer. *Listen* to what God is telling you. Be open to the message.

5. Respond to God from this new perspective, from this new spiritual place. Will it affect your future actions and efforts?

Lectio Divina Guide

This is an alternate form of *lectio* which can be followed at your choice. It is based on *The Song of the Seed* by Macrina Wiederkehr, OSB.[1]

1. Quiet the soul. Do nothing. Take a few minutes to quiet down, sit back (on your soul), and put yourself in the presence of God; become aware of the Spirit within.

2. Reflective reading. Read the word slowly and deliberately; linger with the words and listen.

3. Contemplative sitting. Rest and let the seed of the Word germinate. Wait patiently. Just rest in God. Be present and empty, resting in union with God. You are being held by God in total surrender to the God within you.

4. Meditating. Read the text again. Choose a word or phrase that speaks to you. Work with it; ruminate on it. What is its message for you? You may receive new insights and challenges. Read it a third time if necessary, always slowly.

   Pay attention to feelings and questions that arise. For example, Why does this word or phrase speak to me? What am I feeling? What is God saying to me? Where am I being called to conversion?

5. Prayer. It is time to interface with God. Share what is in your heart with God. Journal. Dance. Draw. Do whatever helps you to pray.

6. Evening. Go over the day. Look at where God has been this day. Pick up the threads of your word or phrase. What feelings arise? Journal.

Lectio Divina **Guide**

You can use Scripture, a life experience, sacred reading, or an icon for *lectio*. Choose a time (preferably the same every day). Allow perhaps twenty minutes or so. Find a quiet place that is not a workplace. If you do choose a workplace, clear it enough to eliminate distractions.

1. Sit still, trying to quiet your mind and body. Close your eyes. Pray to the Spirit to guide you.

2. *Lectio*. Read the Sacred Scripture (or choice of text) slowly once or twice. You might even read it out loud. Stop at a phrase or word that touches you. Write it down if you choose. (If you are using an icon, a work of art, or if you are reflecting on the beauty of something in nature, music, or drama, please focus on it with intense mindfulness and adapt this *lectio* guide to the experience you have chosen.)

3. *Meditatio*. Why does this word or phrase touch you? Think about it, meditate, go deep, reflecting on that word or phrase. Imagine the scene. Make connections with your life. What does the word, phrase, image mean to you? Do not be afraid of your feelings whether "good" or "bad." Do not judge your thoughts by considering: "I shouldn't think this." Write in your journal if you choose.

4. *Oratio*. Prayer. Speak to God about your experience. Listen to what God says to you. To what are you being called? In what way are you being invited to change? Stay in awareness of the presence of God.

5. *Contemplatio*. Contemplate. Rest in your reflection, insight, prayer, feeling. Rest in the presence of God. "Be still and know that I am God."

6. *Compassio*. Compassion. We share this experience of God and send out a prayer of love to a person(s). We may decide to do a specific action for someone—to help or serve someone we know is in need.

Close with a prayer of gratitude.

We read	(*Lectio*)
under the eye of God	(*Meditatio*)
until the heart is touched	(*Oratio*)
and leaps to flame	(*Contemplatio*)

Benedictine Saints and Calendar
(abridged)

Introduction

The list of saints, or saintly people, given in appendix D, is not reflective of, nor even necessarily aligned with, the present Roman Martyrology. It is but a *consciously meager* attempt to whet your appetite and curiosity for Benedictine-oriented men and women of earlier centuries who have lived the Rule in such a way as to be recognized as "holy." Most of the names listed in this calendar can be found in *A Benedictine Martyrology* by Alexius Hoffmann, OSB,[1] which is a revision of the Reverend Peter Lechner's *Ausführliches Martyrologium Des Benedictiner-Ordens und Seiner Verzweigungen.* While this reference reflects other hagiological sources to some extent, the definitive Benedictine Martyrology has yet to be written. The list of Benedictine saints offered here is meant to be not a *scholarly* study of these foremothers and forefathers but a stimulant for reflection about the people, the culture that produced them, and the times they represent.

The people are listed according to the months and dates on which you could choose to celebrate them. Be aware that most of these names will not be a part of your daily Mass/Eucharist even in the form of commemoration or memorial. That is precisely why they are chosen. They will give you someone holy, from the past, with a Benedictine orientation to "look up" on the Internet, in encyclopedias, or in more scholarly, specialized biographies, and can offer you almost daily projects for enlightenment, edification, and intercession. They can form for you a Benedictine community of the "Church Triumphant."

In the future someone may choose to research, clarify, or update lists of Benedictine saints, whether the persons in question were officially canonized or beatified, or have just been held in esteem for their holiness while they lived on earth. You may want to keep your eyes open for such a book or document. Whatever occurs in that regard, we know that we will never have a complete list of the deeply spiritual people who really are saints without recognition—those who have lived the Rule of Benedict faithfully throughout their earthly lives and have gone to their eternal reward, and those others, who even today, walk among us. To all of them we give implied recognition here and gratitude for making our world a better place.

Benedictine Saints

January

1   St. Odilo, abbot of Cluny (died 1049)

   St. William, abbot at Dijon (died 1031)

2   St. Adelard, abbot at Corbie in Picardy (died 827)

   Basil the Great and Gregory Nazianzen, bishops and doctors of the church

3   St. Blitmund, abbot at St. Valery in Picardy (died 650)

4   St. Rigobert, archbishop of Rheims (died ca. 733)

6   St. Peter, abbot of Canterbury (died 606)

8   St. Erhard, bishop of Regensburg (died eighth century)

9   St. Adrian, abbot of St. Peter's at Canterbury (died 710)

10   St. William, archbishop of Bourges (died 1209)

11   St. Taso, abbot of St. Vincent on the river Voltorno (died 729)

12   St. Benedict Biscop, abbot at Wearmouth and Jarrow (died 690)

   St. Aelred, abbot at Rievaulx (Rieval) in England (died 1166)

14   St. Peter Urseolus, doge of Venice (died 987)

   St. Warin, bishop of Sitten (died 1140)

15 Sts. Maurus and Placid, disciples of St. Benedict

St. Ceolwulf, King, monk at Lindisfarne (died 760)

16 St. Fursey, abbot at Lagny, Diocese of Paris (died 650)

Venerable Joanna, sister at Bagno (Bagnorea) (died 1105)

17 Sts. Anthony, Merulus, John, monks at Rome
(died sixth century)

18 Blessed Beatrice of Este, nun at Ferrara (died 1262)

19 St. Wulstan, bishop of Worcester in England (died 1095)

20 St. Maurus, bishop of Cesena in Italy (died 946)

21 St. Meinrad, monk at Einsiedeln (died ca. 863)

22 St. Dominic, abbot at Sora in the former kingdom of Naples
(died 1031)

23 St. Ildephonse, archbishop of Toledo in Spain (died 667)

24 St. Bertram, abbot of St. Quentinin Picardy (died 680)

25 St. Poppo, abbot of Stablo near Liege in Belgium
(died 1048)

26 St. Alberic, abbot of Citeaux (died 1107)

27 St. Theodoric, bishop of Orleans (died 1022)

28 St. Amadeus, bishop of Lausanne in Switzerland (died 1159)

29 St. Gelasius II, pope (died 1119)

30 St. Adelhelm, abbot of St. John at Burgos, Spain (died 1097)

St. Bathildis, queen of France (died 680)

February

 1 St. John, bishop of St. Malo (died 1160)

    St. Clarus, monk of Seligenstadt (died 1043)

 2 St. Lawrence, archbishop of Canterbury (died 619)

 3 St. Ansgar, archbishop of Bremen and Hamburg,
    Apostle of Scandinavia (died 865)

 4 St. Rabanus Maurus, archbishop of Mainz (died 856)

    St. Rembert, archbishop of Bremen and Hamburg (died 888)

 5 St. Berthulph, abbot at Renty in the province of Artois
    (died 705)

    St. Aleidis, abbess of Villich near Bonn (died 1015)

 6 St. Amandus, bishop of Mastricht (died 675)

    St. Ina, king of Wessex, England (died 730)

 7 St. Romuald, founder of the Camaldolese (died 1027)

 8 St. Elfleda, abbess of Whitby, England (died 716)

 9 St. Alto, abbot of Altomuenster, Bavaria (died 760)

    St. Marianus, abbot at Regensburg (died 1088)

10 **St. Scholastica**, sister of St. Benedict (died ca. 543?)

11 St. Benedict, abbot of Aniane (died 821)

    St. Adolph, bishop of Osnabrueck (died 1222)

12 St. Ethelwold, bishop of Lindisfarne in England (died 740)

    St. Humbelina, abbess of Julley, Burgundy, St. Bernard's sister
    (died 1136)

13 St. Gregory II, pope (died 731)

14 St. Antonine, abbot at Sorrento (died 830)

    St. Boniface, martyr, apostle to the Russians (died 1009)

15 St. Walafrid, abbot in Tuscany (died 764)

16 St. Tanco, bishop of Werden in ancient Saxony (died 800)

    Venerable Jaspard de Winck, abbot of St. Denis de Brocheroie
    near Mons in Hainault (died 1630)

17 St. Constabilis, abbot of Cava near Naples (died 1124)

18 St. Helladius, archbishop of Toledo in Spain (died 632)

19 St. Boniface, bishop of Lausanne (died 1266)

20 St. Eucherius, bishop of Orleans (died 743)

21 St. Gumbert, archbishop of Sens (died 675)

22 Blessed Jane Marie Bonomo, abbess at Bassanoin Italy (died 1670)

St. John (Apulus), abbot at Lucca in Italy (died 1055)

23 St. Peter Damian, cardinal, doctor of the church (died 1072)

25 St. Walburga, abbess in Eichstaett, Bavaria (died 779)

Venerable Mary Adeodata, abbess in Malta (died 1855)

26 Blessed Mechtildis, oblate at Spanheim (died 1154)

27 St. Leander, archbishop of Seville, Spain (died 601)

28 St. Herbert, abbot of Wearmouth and Jarrow (died eighth century)

29 St. Oswald, archbishop of York (died 992)

March

1   St. Rudesind, bishop at Duma in Portugal (died 977)

2   St. Suitbert, bishop, apostle of Frisia (died 713)

3   St. Cunegundis, empress of Germany (died 1039)

   St. Anselm, abbot of Nonantula in Italy (died 803)

4   St. Peter, bishop of Policastro, Italy (died 1118)

5   Venerable Hincmar, abbot of St. Remigius at Rheims (died 967)

6   St. Kyneburga, abbess in England (died seventh century)

7   St. Esterwin, abbot at Wearmouth in England (died 685)

8   St. Veremund, abbot of Gerace (died 1092)

9   *St. Frances of Rome*, oblate, patroness of oblates (died 1440)

10   St. Aemilian, abbot at Lagny near Paris (died 676)

11   St. Vincent, abbot of St. Claudius in Spain, Martyr (died 584)

   St. Aurea, nun in Spain (died 1100)

12   St. Gregory the Great, pope, doctor of the church who wrote about St. Benedict (died 604)

   St. Elphege, bishop of Winchester (died 951)

13   St. Ramirus and companions, martyrs, monks in Spain (died 584)

14   Blessed Mathildis, empress of Germany (died 968)

15   St. Raymond, abbot of Fitero in Spain (died 1163)

17   St. Gertrude, abbess of Nivelle in Brabant (died 659)

18   St. Anselm, bishop of Lucca in Italy (died 1086)

20   St. Cuthbert, bishop of Lindisfarne in England (died 687)

21   **St. Benedict**, patriarch of Western monks (died 547)

22   Venerable Conrad, abbot of Mondsee, Diocese of Salzburg (died 1145)

24   St. Aldemar, abbot of Bocchianico in Italy (died 1087)

   Blessed Bertha, abbess in Tuscany (died 1163)

26 St. Ludger, bishop of Muenster (died 809)

27 St. Rupert, bishop of Salzburg, apostle of Bavaria (died 623)

28 St. Stephen Harding, third abbot of Citeaux, one of the founders of the Cistercians (died 1134)

29 Venerable Stephen X, pope, abbot at Monte Cassino (died 1058)

30 St. Zosimus, bishop of Syracuse in Sicily (died 660)

31 St. Guido, abbot at Pomposa in Italy (died 1046)

April

1 St. Hugh (Hugo), bishop of Grenoble (died 1132)

St. Procopius, abbot at Prague (died 1053)

2 St. Ebba, abbess of Coldingham in Scotland (died 870)

3 St. Richard, bishop of Chichester (died 1253)

4 Venerable Maurus Xavier Herbst, abbot of Plankstetten (died 1757)

5 St. Gerald, founder and abbot of Sauve-Majeure in Aquitaine (died 1095)

St. Ethelburga, abbess in England (died 647)

7 St. Eberhard, monk at Schauffhausen in Switzerland (died 1075)

8 St. Walter, abbot at Pontoise in France (died 1099)

9 St. Hugo, archbishop of Rouen (died 730)

12 St. Alferius, abbot of Cava in Italy (died 1050)

13 Blessed Ida, nun of Rosenthal in Belgium (died 1300)

14 St. Bernard, abbot, founder of the congregation of Tiron in France (died 1117)

15 Venerable Wolbert, abbot of Deutz near Cologne (died 1021)

16 St. Fructuosus, monk and archbishop of Braga in Portugal (died 665)

17 St. Robert, founder and abbot of Chaise-Dieu in France (died 1076)

19 St. Leo IX, pope (died 1054)

St. Elphege, archbishop of Canterbury (died 1012)

20 St. Wolbodo, bishop of Liege in Belgium (died 1021)

St. Hildegundis, nun of Schoenau near Heidelberg (died 1188)

21 St. Anselm, archbishop of Canterbury, doctor of the church (died 1109)

22 Venerable Antonia of Orleans-Longueville, foundress of Notre Dame du Calvaire (died 1618)

23 St. Adelbert, bishop of Prague, martyr, apostle of Prussia (died 997)

24 St. Mellitus, archbishop of Canterbury (died 624)

25 St. Ermin, abbot of Lobbe in Belgium (died 737)

St. Franca, abbess of Pittoli in Italy (died 1218)

26 St. Paschasius Radbertus, abbot of Corbie in France (died 865)

28 Venerable John de la Barriere, founder, abbot of Notre Dame des Feuillants (died 1600)

29 St. Hugo the Great, abbot of Cluny (died 1109)

St. Robert, abbot and founder of Cistercians (died 1110)

30 St. Erconwald, bishop of London (died 690)

St. Suitbert, bishop of Werden, apostle to Saxony (died 807)

May

1 Blessed Margaret of Amelia, abbess in Italy (died 1666)

2 Blessed Mafalda, queen of Castile and Cistercian nun (died 1252)

4 St. Godhard, bishop of Hildesheim in Germany (died 1038)

St. Ethelred, king of Mercia (died 716)

5 St. Maurontius, abbot of Breuil (died 701)

6 St. Petronax, abbot of Monte Cassino (died 750)

7 St. John of Beverley, archbishop of York (died 721)

8 St. Peter, archbishop of Tarantasia in Savoy (died 1174)

9 St. Gregory, cardinal bishop of Ostia, abbot in Rome (died 1044)

10 Blessed Beatrice of Este, abbess of Gemmula (died 1226)

11 St. Majolus, abbot of Cluny (died 994)

12 St. Rictrudis, abbess at Marchiennes in Flanders (died 688)

13 All saints whose relics are preserved in Benedictine churches

14 St. Paschal I, pope (died 824)

16 St. Herchantrudis, nun of Faremoutier in France (died 650)

18 Venerable Peter, abbot of Clairvaux (died 1186)

19 St. Peter Celestine, pope, founder of Celestines (died 1296)

St. Dunstan, archbishop of Canterbury (died 988)

21 St. Godric, oblate at Durham (died 1170)

22 St. Romanus, abbot of Fontrouge (died ca. 545)

St. John, abbot of St. John's at Parma, Italy (died 982)

23 St. Guibert, monk of Gemblours in Brabant (died 962)

25 St. Boniface IV, pope (died 615)

St. Gregory VII, pope (died 1085)

St. Aldhelm, bishop of Sherburne in England (died 709)

26 St. Augustine, bishop of Canterbury, apostle of England
    (died 607)

27 St. Bede the Venerable, monk, doctor of the church
    (died 735)

28 St. William, monk of Valgellon in Languedoc (died 812)

31 St. Benedict, abbot at Chiusa in the diocese of Turin
    (died 1091)

June

1 St. Eneco (Inigo), abbot at Onna in Old Castile (died 1057)

3 St. Isaac, monk in Cordova, martyr (died 851)
   Venerable Hildeburg, nun at Pontoise (died 1115)

4 St. Peter de Bono, monk of Cluny (died 1441)
   Venerable Werner, abbot of Wiblingen near Ulm (died 1126)

5 St. Boniface, archbishop of Mainz, apostle of Germany, martyr (died 755)

6 St. Claudius, archbishop of Besancon (died 693)

7 St. Peter and companions, monks at Cordova, martyrs (died 851)
   St. Robert, abbot of Newminster in England (died 1159)

9 St. George, monk at Vabres in France (died 880)

10 St. Bardo, archbishop of Mainz (died 1051)

11 Blessed Aleidis (Adelaide), nun near Scarbeke in Brabant (died 1250)

12 St. Leo III, pope (died 816)
   Sts. Marinus, Zimius, and Vimius, oblates at Regensburg (died eleventh century)

14 Sts. Anastasius, Felix, and Digna, martyrs at Cordova (died 853)
   St. Basil the Great, founder of Eastern monasticism (died 379)

15 St. Landelin, abbot of Crespin in Hainaut (died 686)

16 St. Benno, bishop of Meissen, patron saint of Bavaria (died 1106)

17 St. Botulph, abbot in England (died 655)

18 St. Elizabeth, prioress of Schoenau near Bingen (died 1165)

19 St. Hildegrim, bishop of Halberstadt, abbot of Werden (died 827)

20 St. John of Matera, abbot of Pulsano (died 1139)

21 St. Leutfrid, abbot of Lacroix in Normandy (died 738)

22 St. Eberhard, archbishop of Salzburg (died 1164)

23 St. Ediltrude, abbess at Ely (died 679)

24 St. Eric, monk of St. Germain at Auxerre (died 924)

25 St. William, founder of the congregation of Monte Vergine in Italy (died 1142)

26 St. Rudolph, bishop of Gubbio in Italy (died 1063)

27 Venerable Daniel, abbot of Schoenau near Heidelberg (died ca. 1290)

28 Venerable Notker Labeo, abbot of St. Gall's in Switzerland (died 1022)

29 Blessed Salome, oblate at Niederaltaich (date of death unknown)

30 Blessed Philip Powell, monk of Douay, martyr (died 1646)

July

1   St. Theobald, oblate at Vangadizza (died 1066)

2   St. Swithin, bishop of Winchester (died 862)

3   St. Lidanus of Antino, abbot at Sezza, Italy (died 1118)

4   St. Odo the Good, archbishop of Canterbury (died 961)

    Blessed William, abbot of Hirschau in Wuerttemberg (died 1091)

5   Blessed Angelo de Masaccio, monk in Italy, martyr (died 1458)

    Venerable Martha, nun in Belgium (died thirteenth century)

6   Blessed Mary Rose, nun at Caderousse, martyr (died 1794)

    St. Thomas More, chancellor of England, model for all oblates, martyr (died 1534)

7   St. Willibald, bishop of Eichstaett in Bavaria (died 786)

8   Blessed Eugene III, pope (died 1153)

9   St. Agilolf, archbishop of Cologne, martyr (died 770)

10 St. Amalberga, nun at Maubeuge in Belgium (died 690)

11 **Solemnity of St. Benedict**

    Blessed Magdalen, nun at Avignon, martyr (died 1794)

12 St. John Gualbert, founder of the Congregation of Vallombrosa (died 1073)

13 St. Mildred, abbess of Minstrey (died 700)

14 St. Vincent, monk of Soignies in Hainaut (died 677)

15 *St. Henry II*, emperor, patron of oblates (died 1024)

    St. David, abbot in Sweden (died 1060)

16 Blessed Irmengard, abbess of Frauen-Chiemsee in Bavaria (died 866)

17 St. Leo IV, pope (died 855)

18 St. Bruno, bishop of Segni in Italy (died 1123)

19 St. Ambrose Autpert, abbot of St. Vincent on the Voltorno (died 779)

20   St. Ansegisus, abbot at Fontenelle, Diocese of Rouen
      (died 834)

21   Sts. John and Benignus, twin brothers, monks of Marmoutier
      (or Movenmoutier) (died 707)

22   St. Wandrille, abbot at Fontenelle (died 666)

23   St. Offa, abbess of St. Peter's in Benevento, Italy (died 1070)

24   St. Godo, abbot at Oye (died ca. 690)

25   St. Clodesindis, abbess at Metz (died ca. 610)

26   St. Simeon, oblate at Polirone in Italy (died 1016)

27   St. Berthold, abbot of Steyergarsten in Austria (died 1142)

28   Blessed Jerome, monk at Prague (died 1440)

29   Blessed Urban II, pope (died 1099)

30   St. Tatwin, archbishop of Canterbury (died 734)

31   St. Neot, abbot/founder of St. Neot's (died 877)

August

1 St. Ethelwold, bishop of Winchester (died 984)

2 St. Peter, bishop of Osma in Spain (died 1109)

3 St. Peter, bishop of Anagni, Italy (died 1105)

4 Venerable Thomas Lombard, monk in Ireland (died 1604)

5 Venerable John Feckenham, last abbot of Westminster (died 1585)

6 St. Stephen, abbot at Cardenna, and two hundred monks, martyrs in Spain (died 872)

7 Blessed Jordan Forzate, abbot at Padua (died 1240)

8 St. Famian, monk and hermit (died 1150)

9 St. Maurilius, archbishop of Rouen (died 1076)

10 St. Malchus, bishop of Lismore in Ireland (died 1150)

11 St. Agilberta, abbess of Jouarre, Diocese of Meaux (died seventh century)

12 St. Cecilia, abbess of Remiremont (died 670)

13 Sts. Ludolph (died 983) and Druthmar (died 1046), abbots of New Corvey in Westphalia

14 Blessed Eberhard, abbot of Einsiedeln (died 958)

15 St. Arnulph, bishop of Soissons, founder of Aldenburg monastery (died 1087)

16 Blessed Lawrence, oblate at Subiaco (died 1243)
    Venerable Margaret, abbess of Val de Grace (died 1626)

17 St. Donatus, monk of Monte Vergine in Italy (died 1198)

18 Blessed Balderic, abbot at Mountfaucon (died 640)

19 St. Berthulph, abbot of Bobbio (died 640)

20 St. Bernard, abbot of Clairvaux, doctor of the church (died 1153)

21 Blessed Bernard Tolomei, founder of the Olivetans (died 1348)

22 St. Sigfrid, abbot of Wearmouth (died 689)

23 St. Ascelina, nun at Boulencourt in Champagne (died 1195)

24 Blessed Theodoric, abbot of St. Hubert at Andaine (died 1087)

25 St. Gregory, abbot and bishop of Utrecht (died 776)

26 Blessed John Bassandus, provincial of the Celestines
     (died 1445)

27 St. Ebbo, archbishop of Sens in France (died 774)

28 St. Alfric, archbishop of Canterbury (died 1006)

29 St. Sebbi, king of Essex (died 694)

30 St. Bononius, abbot of Lucedio in Piedmont (died 1026)

31 St. Amatus, bishop of Nusco in former kingdom of Naples
     (died 1193)

September

1   Blessed Juliana, abbess at St. Blasius in Venice (died 1262)

2   Venerable Anthony de Winghe, abbot of Liessies in Hainaut (died 1637)

3   St. Remaclus, bishop of Mastricht (died 664)

4   Venerable Simon, abbot of St. Peter at Caziac (died 1160)

5   St. Bertin, abbot of Sithiu in Artois (died 709)

6   St. Magnus, abbot at Fuessen in the Allgaeu (died 660)

7   St. John, bishop of Gubbio in Italy (died 1106)

8   St. Disibod, bishop and abbot (died ca. 700)

9   St. Corbinian, bishop of Freising, patron saint of that Bavarian diocese (died 730)

10 Blessed Edward Ambrose Barlow, monk at Douay, martyr (died 1641)

11 St. Sperandea, abbess in Italy (died 1276)

12 Blessed Thesaurus Beccheria, cardinal (died 1258)

13 St. Amatus, bishop of Sitten (died 690)

14 Blessed Leoteric, monk at Cormery near Tours (died 1099)

15 St. Rithbert, abbot of St. Valery in the Diocese of Amiens (died ca. 700)

16 Blessed Victor III, pope (died 1087)

17 St. Lambert, bishop of Mastricht, martyr (died 708)

    St. Hildegard, abbess at Bingen (died 1179)

18 St. Richardis, empress, founder of monastery of Andlau (died 896)

19 Venerable Louis Barbo, abbot and bishop of Treviso in Italy (died 1443)

20 Blessed John Eustachius, abbot of Jardinet in Belgium (died 1441)

21 Venerable Paul, deacon at Monte Cassino (died 1033)

22   Blessed Maurice, abbot in Brittany (died 1215)

23   Blessed Guido, abbot of Chalis (died 1130)

24   St. Gerard Sagredo, apostle of Hungary, martyr (died 1046)

25   St. Ceolfrid, abbot of Wearmouth and Jarrow in England
     (died 716)

26   St. John de Meda, founder of the Humiliati (died 1159)

27   St. Bonfilius, bishop of Foligno in Italy (died 1115)

     St. Hiltrudis, nun of Liessies in Hainaut (died ca. 790)

28   St. Thiemo, archbishop of Salzburg (died 1101)

     St. Lioba, abbess of Bischofsheim on the Tauber (died 779)

29   St. Ludwin, archbishop of Trier (died 713)

30   St. Simon, monk of Cluny (died 1080)

     St. Eusebia, abbess of St. Cyricus at Marseilles (died 732)

October

1   St. Bavo, monk at St. Peter's in Ghent in Flanders (died 654)

2   St. Leodegar (Leger), bishop of Autun, martyr (died 678)

3   St. Gerard, abbot of Brogne in Belgium (died 959)

4   St. Aurea, abbess at Paris (died 959)

5   St. Placid, disciple of St. Benedict (died ca. 542 or 546 according to Lechner)

6   St. Adalbero, bishop of Augsburg (died 909)

7   St. Ositha, abbess at Chich, martyr (died 653)

8   Blessed Compagnus, monk at Padua (died 1264)

9   Blessed Gunther, monk and hermit at Niederaltaich in Bavaria (died 1045)

10 St. Paulinus, archbishop of York (died 644)

11 St. Ethelburga, abbess of Barking in England (died 705)

12 St. Wilfrid, archbishop of York (died 709)

13 St. Simpert, bishop of Augsburg (died 807)

14 St. Burkard, bishop of Wuerzburg (died 752)

15 St. Hedwig, duchess of Silesia and Poland, oblate (died 1243)

St. Thecla, abbess at Kitzingen (died ca. 750)

16 St. Gall, abbot, founder of St. Gall's in Switzerland (died 646)

17 St. Anstrudis, abbess of St. John at Laon (died 688)

18 Venerable Benno, bishop of Hamburg, fifth apostle of the Wends (died 1190)

19 St. Frideswida, abbess at Oxford (died 790)

20 St. Wendelin, abbot of Tholey in the Diocese of Trier (died 650)

21 St. Wimo, bishop of Bremen, apostle to Goths (died 936)

22 St. Bertharius, abbot of Monte Cassino, martyr (died 884)

23 St. Bernard, bishop of Vich in Spain (died 1243)

24 St. Martin, abbot of Vertou in Brittany (died 601)

25 St. Hildemarca, abbess at Fecamp in Normandy (died 670)

26 St. Albuin, bishop of Fritzlar (died 787)

27 St. Tetta, abbess of the double monastery of Winborn in England (died 760)

29 St. Elfleda, abbess of Ramsey in England (died 930)

30 St. Egelnoth the Good, archbishop of Canterbury (died 1038)

31 St. Wolfgang, bishop of Regensburg (died 994)

November

1   St. Genesius, archbishop of Lyons in France (died 668)

2   St. Benno, founder of Clynnog Fawr (died ca. 620)

3   St. Pirmin, bishop, founder and restorer of several abbeys (died 758)

4   St. Bertilia, abbess of Chelles near Paris (died 692)

5   St. Malachy, archbishop of Armagh in Ireland (died 1148)

6   St. Winoc, abbot of Wornhout in Flanders (died 717)

7   St. Willibrord, bishop of Utrecht, apostle of Frisia (died 738)

8   St. Godfrey, bishop of Amiens (died 1118)

9   Venerable Henry, bishop of Luebeck (died 1184)

10 St. Justus, archbishop of Canterbury (died 627)

11 Venerable Sergius, archbishop of Damascus (died 981)

12 St. Emilian, abbot of St. Millan de Cogolla in Spain (died 574)

13 All saints of the Benedictine Order

St. Abbo, abbot of Fleury, martyr (died 1004)

14 All souls of the Benedictine Order

15 St. Fintan, monk of Rheinau (died 878)

16 St. Othmar, abbot of St. Gall's in Switzerland (died 759)

17 St. Gertrude the Great, nun at Helfta in Saxony (died 1302)

18 St. Odo, abbot of Cluny (died 942)

19 St. Mechtildis, nun at Helfta (died 1298)

20 St. Bernward, bishop of Hildesheim (died 1022)

21 Presentation of Blessed Virgin Mary, patronal feast of the oblates

Blessed Gelasius O'Cullenan, abbot at Boyle, martyr (died 1584)

22 Blessed John Thorn and Blessed Roger James, monks of Glastonbury, martyrs (died 1539)

23   St. Guido, abbot at Casauria in Italy (died 1045)

24   Blessed Balsamus, abbot of Cava in Italy (died 1232)

25   Blessed Tussanus, prior at Cluny in France (died 1420)

26   St. Sylvester, founder of the Sylvestrine Benedictines
      (died 1267)

27   St. Virgil, archbishop of Salzburg (died 780)

28   St. Germanus, prior of Taloire (died eleventh century)

29   St. Radbod, bishop of Utrecht (died 918)

30   St. Angelo, abbot at Palermo (died 1380)

December

1 Blessed Richard Whiting, Blessed Hugh Faringdon, Blessed John Beach, abbots in England, martyrs (died 1539)

2 Blessed Oderisius, abbot of Monte Cassino, cardinal (died 1105)

3 St. Galganus, hermit (died 1181)

4 St. Bernard, bishop of Parma, cardinal (died 1133)

5 St. Gerard, archbishop of Braga in Portugal (died 1109)

6 Blessed Nicholas, abbot at Vaucelles in the Diocese of Cambrai (died 1163)

7 St. Fara, foundress and abbess of Faremoutier (died 655)

8 St. Romaric, abbot of Remiremont (died 653)

9 St. Wulfhildis, abbess at Barking in England (died 990)

10 Blessed John Roberts, monk of Compostella, martyr (died 1610)

11 Blessed Ida of Nivelle, nun at Rameige in Brabant (died 1231)

   St. Tato, abbot of St. Vincent's on the Voltorno (died 739)

12 St. Walaric, founder of St. Valery (died 622)

13 St. Odilia, abbess of Hohenburg in Alsace (died 720)

14 St. Agnellus, abbot at Naples (died 596)

15 Blessed Raynald, bishop of Nocera in Umbria (died 1225)

16 St. Ado, archbishop of Vienne (died 875)

   St. Adelaide, empress, founder and endower of monasteries (died 999)

17 St. Sturmius, abbot at Fulda (died 779)

18 St. Wunibald, abbot at Heidenheim in the Diocese of Eichstaett (died 760)

19 Blessed Urban V, pope (died 1370)

20 St. Dominic, abbot at Silos in Spain (died 1073)

21 Venerable Baudacharius, monk at Bobbio in Italy (died 650)

22   St. Jutta, abbess at Diesenberg near Mainz (died 1136)

23   Venerable Agnes, oblate, widow of Emperor Henry III
(died 1077)

24   St. Adela, abbess at Pfalzel on the Moselle (died 734)

25   Blessed Peter the Venerable, abbot of Cluny (died 1157)

26   Venerable Adelard, monk of Hirschauin in Wuerttemberg
(died 924)

27   St. Edburga, nun at Winchester (died 985)

28   Venerable Hucbald, monk of St. Peter's at Orbains
(died tenth century)

29   St. Thomas a Becket, archbishop of Canterbury, martyr
(died 1170)

30   Blessed Ralph, abbot at Vaucelles near Cambrai (died 1151)

31   Blessed Peter, abbot of Subiaco (died 1103)

The Medal of Saint Benedict

Oblate candidates at Saint Benedict's Monastery receive the Benedictine medal on the day they are received as candidates. This medal is a powerful sacramental and once we understand the inscriptions and images given us on this medal, it can be a true source of meditation, prayer, and a reminder of God's protection and aid in our lives.

History of the Benedictine Medal

Saint Benedict had a deep faith in the power of the cross of Christ. In the *Dialogues*, Saint Gregory the Great relates the miracles Benedict performed when he invoked that power. Two of those miracles are alluded to and represented on the front of the Benedictine medal and will be described in the explanation of the symbols. Though there were Benedictine medals in earlier centuries, for our purposes we will describe the Jubilee Medal, first struck in 1880 to mark the 1400th anniversary of the birth of Saint Benedict. This medal's process was supervised by the monks of Monte Cassino (Italy), the abbey founded by Saint Benedict and where he lived most of his life, where he wrote the Rule, and where he died in AD 543.

Front of the Jubilee Medal

On the front of the medal and in its center one sees the image of Saint Benedict who holds a cross in his right hand and the Rule in the left. All Christians are aware of the salvific power of the cross of Christ and history attests to the role the Benedictines played in the Christianization and civilization of Europe.

To the lower right of Benedict there is the poisoned cup with a snake inside. This is a reference to St. Gregory's narration about the monks who had asked Benedict to be their abbot, then, finding him too strict for their liking, they gave him a cup of poisoned wine to drink. When Benedict made the sign of the cross over the cup before drinking from it, it shattered "as if a stone had been thrown at it."

To the lower left of Benedict's image is a raven carrying away a loaf of bread that had been poisoned and sent to Benedict by one of his enemies.

On each side of Benedict (above the cup and the raven) we read "*Crux S. Patris Benedicti,*" which translates, "The Cross of our Holy Father Benedict."

Circling the medal at the perimeter are the Latin words "*Eius in obitu nostro praesentia muniamur.*" In translation: "May we be strengthened by his presence in the hour of our death." (Or "At our death may we be fortified by his presence.") It is interesting to note that Saint Benedict is a patron of the dying or, to phrase it differently, a patron of a happy death. At Monte Cassino there is a sculpture that depicts Benedict's own death. He stands with his arms raised to heaven and is literally supported by his monastic brothers as he breathes his last, after having received the Holy Eucharist.

Bronze group of the Dying Benedict at Monte Cassino. Sculptor: A. Selva, 1952. Photo courtesy of Wikimedia Commons/Radomil.

Beneath Benedict's feet on the front of the medal are the words "ex SM Casino MDCCCLXXX," which translate as, "from holy Monte Cassino, 1880," referring to the year and place where the Jubilee Medal was struck.[1]

Back of the Jubilee Medal

The cross is central on the back of the medal. The vertical beam bears the letters "CSSML" and the horizontal beam reads "NDSMD." In Latin the words flow rhythmically as:

> *Crux sacra sit mihi lux!* (vertical arm)
> *Nunquam draco sit mihi dux!*
> (horizontal arm)

The English translation is:

> May the holy cross be my light!
> May the dragon never be my guide!

In the angles of the cross, and circled, are the letters:

> CSPB, which stand for, "*Crux Sancti Patris Benedicti*"

That is:

> "The cross of our Holy Father Benedict."

Above the vertical arm of the cross we read "*pax*," which means "peace." "Peace" has been a Benedictine motto and value for centuries.

The outer circle of the medal contains these letters, which stand for the Latin words related to exorcism:

V R S N S M V—S M Q L I V B

(Latin)	(English)
Vade retro Satana!	Be gone Satan!
Nunquam suade mihi vana!	Never tempt me with your vanities!
Sunt mala quae libas.	What you offer me is evil.
Ipse venena bibas!	Drink the poison yourself![2]

Use of Saint Benedict's Medal

Any use of Saint Benedict's medal should include the faith-filled intention of invoking God's aid, protection, and blessings through the intercession of Saint Benedict. The medal is a sacramental of the church and may be put on a chain and worn around the neck or may be attached to another religious article such as the rosary. It may be carried in a purse, pocket, attaché case, or suitcase. Some people have placed it in the foundations of buildings, hung it on the walls of their homes, or placed it in their automobiles. Its presence, whether on the person or on property, can be a spiritual reminder and experience recalling us to the God who made us and the powerful intercessor we possess in Saint Benedict.

After reading the above explanation of the images, symbols, and text-represented letters present on Saint Benedict's medal, one can realize some of the purposes for which this medal has been known and is used today. It is and has been efficacious as:

(1) an exorcism against Satan and as a help to ward off the temptations of the devil;
(2) assistance in the hour of death and aid in a good and (even) holy death;
(3) an aid in obtaining the grace of conversion;
(4) a protection against contagious diseases and bodily suffering;
(5) a protection against storms on land or sea;
(6) a concrete reminder of the cross of Christ and its power;
(7) a prayer for peace, both personal and worldwide.[3]

Blessing of the Medal of Saint Benedict

Saint Benedict medals may be blessed by any priest or deacon using this form:

℣. Our help is in the name of the Lord.
℟. Who made heaven and earth.

In the name of God the Father <+> almighty, who made heaven and earth, the seas and all that is in them, I exorcise these medals against the power and attacks of the evil one. May all who use these medals devoutly be blessed with health of soul and body. In the name of the Father <+> almighty, of the Son <+> Jesus Christ our Lord, and of the Holy <+> Spirit the Paraclete, and in the love of the same Lord Jesus Christ who will come on the last day to judge the living and the dead, and the world by fire. Amen.

Let us pray. Almighty God, the boundless source of all good things, we humbly ask that, through the intercession of St. Benedict, you pour out your blessings <+> upon these medals. May those who use them devoutly and earnestly strive to perform good works, be blessed by you with health of soul and body, the grace of a holy life, and remission of the temporal punishment due to sin.

May they also, with the help of your merciful love, resist the temptation of the evil one and strive to exercise true charity and justice toward all, so that one day they may appear sinless and holy in your sight. This we ask through Christ our Lord. Amen.

The medals are then sprinkled with holy water.[4]

Prayers Appropriate to the Medal's Usage

Prayer to St. Benedict

Beloved, St. Benedict, full of wisdom and grace, please intercede for me to our loving God. As I am faced with the challenges, sorrows, and joys of daily living I ask that your loving heart plead for the graces, blessings, and strength I need to shun evil and do good. Please obtain for me from God all the favors, healing, and wisdom I need as I attend to my daily tasks in the spirit of Christ. You were so close to God and lived the Gospel message with love, and compassion, consolation, and assistance to all who had recourse to you. Because of that I am confident that you will hear my prayer and ask God to obtain for me the special grace and favor for which I plead. (State your request here.)

Great and holy Benedict, please assist me in all my efforts to live my life faithful to God and God's will. Through your intercession and God's loving kindness may I continue to strive for and finally reach the eternal happiness of heaven. I ask all in Jesus' name. Amen.

Prayer for a Happy Death (traditional Benedictine prayer)

O Holy Father, Benedict, blessed by God both in grace and in name, who, while standing in prayer, with your hands raised to heaven did most happily yield your angelic spirit into the hands of your creator, and have promised zealously to defend against all the snares of the enemy in the last struggle of death, those who shall daily remind you of your glorious departure and your heavenly joys; protect me, I beseech you, O glorious father, this day and every day, by your holy blessing, that I may never be separated from our dear Lord, from the society of yourself, and of all the blessed. Through the same Christ our Lord. Amen.[5]

Prayer for Peace

St. Benedict, you were a man of peace. You walked the paths of peace your whole life long and led all who came to you into the ways of peace. Help us, St. Benedict, to achieve peace: peace in our hearts, peace in our homes, peace in our sorely troubled world. Through your powerful intercession with God, help us to be peacemakers. Aid us to work for peace, to take the first step in ending bitterness, to be the first to hold out our hands in friendship and forgiveness. Beg God to let peace permeate our lives so that they may be lived in God's grace and love. And at the end of our lives obtain for us the reward of the peacemakers, the eternal blessed vision of God in heaven. Amen.[6]

Example of a Monastery's Spiritual Support for Oblates

Saint Benedict's Monastery, St. Joseph, Minnesota, offers the following spiritual support for its oblates. At present, an oblate advisory team meets with the director and assistant director of oblates to continue to discern how best to serve the Saint Benedict oblates. The following list will expand as new ideas are implemented:

1. Oblates are remembered daily at Evening Prayer.

2. Oblates are invited to the Spirituality Center on campus for spiritual enrichment, including retreats, workshops, spiritual direction, and prayer.

3. Oblates are invited, encouraged, and welcomed to attend liturgical services at the monastery: Divine Office, Eucharist, and special occasions.

4. Oblate Sundays are held four times a year at the monastery. All candidates and oblates are invited. The day includes Eucharist, dining with the sisters, and a type of enrichment/educational program in the form of a lecture or presentation of a specific type.

5. There is a yearly Oblate Renewal Day at the monastery, during which new candidates are received, former candidates make their final commitment, and all oblates present renew their promises. Oblates share in Morning Prayer and Eucharist and dine with the sisters. During this day there is a presentation to inform and enrich the participants and there is also free time for oblates to socialize and visit various spaces on campus, including the museum and bookstore. At

special times there is a nationally or internationally known speaker.

6. Oblates are able to attend the Monastic Institute and interact with monastics and other oblates from the United States and around the world.

7. Oblates receive a newsletter offering such things as reflection on the Rule, meditations, articles on the history of Saint Benedict's Monastery, articles by oblates attesting to how they live the life, invitations to monastery events, book reviews, notification of the death of an oblate and of those who need prayers, and more.

8. Oblates are invited to attend a discussion group that meets once a month in their area. They pray together, share *lectio*, discuss the book chosen by the group, and then socialize.

9. The monastery has a specific location on campus which provides the oblates with a lounge and a spiritual library of their own.

10. New discussion groups may form in various areas as the geographical picture dictates.

11. There is a group of oblates who connect frequently online.

12. There are some oblates who companion homebound oblates or those who live a considerable distance from the monastery and cannot participate in activities that are connected to their oblate family and monastery. Companioning is done via telephone or the communication of mutual choice.

13. Oblates have the opportunity to participate in the meetings of the North American Association of Benedictine Oblate Directors (NAABOD).

14. Oblates can choose to participate in the Oblates of Saint Benedict's Ministry of Prayer.

When you decide to become an oblate at the monastery of your choice, you will quickly access the types of spiritual support it offers.

Websites for Information on Benedictines and Oblates

Over time these addresses may change or the site may be removed. These are but suggestions to get you started.

Benedictines

1. www.osb.org (General information)
2. www.sbm.osb.org (Saint Benedict's Monastery)
3. www.saintjohnsabbey.org/
4. http://www.saintvincentarchabbey.org

Liturgy of the Hours

1. www.newadvent.org
2. www.universalis.com/
3. www.ebreviary.com
4. www.catholicliturgy.com/index.cfm
5. www.liturgyofthehours.org
6. www.idahomonks.org/sect702.htm
7. www.ewtn.com/expert/answers/breviary.htm
8. www.divineoffice.org

Lectio Divina

1. www.valyermo.com/ld-art.html
2. www.idahomonks.org/sect810.htm
3. www.ocarm.org/en/content/lectio/what-lectio-divina
4. www.prayerfoundation.org/lectio_divina.htm

Oblate Resources

1. www.oblatebooks.com
2. www.litpress.org

General Catholic

1. The Vatican: www.vatican.va/

How to Form
a New Oblate Discussion Group

1. Determine the number of people in your geographical area who are oblates or oblate candidates of your monastery.

2. Contact them to ascertain their level of interest in forming a group.

3. Report the information to the director of oblates at your monastery.

4. Meet with the director or communicate with her or him regarding the:

   1. Process for a meeting
   2. Prayer sheets
   3. Spiritual books recommended
   4. Extracurriculars and/or questions

5. Set the date and location for meeting on a regular basis.

6. Invite the oblate director, the assistant director, or the director's representative to be present in the initial stages, and at least occasionally once the group has a strong foundation.

7. Share any exciting news with the oblate director or assistant so the information can be shared with the readers of the oblate newsletter or added to other relevant monastery communications.

Notes

Chapter 2—pages 4–19

1. Pope Gregory the Great, *The Dialogues*, book 2: *The Life and Miracles of St. Benedict*, trans. Odo J. Zimmermann and Benedict R. Avery (Collegeville, MN: Liturgical Press, 1949), 16.

2. *Rule of St. Benedict 1980*, ed. Timothy Fry (Collegeville, MN: Liturgical Press, 1981). All subsequent references to the Rule of Benedict will be from this edition. All italics are from the original, noting direct quotes from Scripture or Benedict's own emphasis.

3. Rita McClain Tybor, "Prayer and Work in the Light of Dorothy Day," *Benedict in the World: Portraits of Monastic Oblates*, ed. Linda Kulzer and Roberta Bondi (Collegeville, MN: Liturgical Press, 2002), 60.

4. Ibid., 65.

5. Ibid., 64.

6. Lucie R. Johnson, "St. Benedict and the Maritains," *Benedict in the World* (Collegeville, MN: Liturgical Press, 2002), 145.

7. Ibid., 151.

8. "Beatification Process for Jacques and Raissa Maritain Could Begin," *Rome Reports*, February 8, 2011, http://www.romereports.com/palio/beatification-process-for-jacques-and-raissa-maritain-could-begin-english-3515.html.

9. Kathleen O'Flaherty quoting from Claudel's "Magnificat" in *Paul Claudel and the Tidings Brought to Mary* (Oxford: Cork University Press, 1948), 14.

10. Louis Chaigne, quoting Claudel in *Paul Claudel: The Man and the Mystic* (New York: Appleton-Century-Crofts, Inc., 1961), 4.

11. Ibid.

12. Ibid., 81.

13. Ibid., 10.

14. Ibid., 15.

15. Paul Claudel, *Letters to a Doubter* (New York: Albert and Charles Boni, 1927), 45.

16. Chaigne, quoting Barrault in *Paul Claudel: The Man and the Mystic*, 276.

17. Claudel, *Letters to a Doubter*, 81.

18. Esther de Waal, *Seeking God: The Way of St. Benedict* (Collegeville, MN: Liturgical Press, 1984), 12.

19. Jane Tomaine, *St. Benedict's Toolbox: The Nuts and Bolts of Everyday Benedictine Living* (Harrisburg, PA: Morehouse Publishing, 2005), 5.

20. Ibid., 22.

21. Tomaine, quoting Will Derkse in *St. Benedict's Toolbox*, 24.

22. Katherine Howard, *Praying with Benedict: Companions for the Journey* (Winona, MN: Saint Mary's Press, 1996), 29.

23. Joan Chittister, *The Rule of Benedict: Insights for the Ages* (New York: Crossroad, 1992), 19.

24. Roberta Bondi, "Foreword: On Being a Benedictine Oblate," in *Benedict in the World: Portraits of Monastic Oblates*, ed. Linda Kulzer and Roberta Bondi (Collegeville, MN: Liturgical Press, 2002), vi.

25. Ibid., vii.

26. Gerald W. Schlabach, "Stability in the World: An Oblate's Reflection," para. 9, 10, http://personal2.stthomas.edu/gwschlabach/docs/oblates.htm.

27. Margaret Guenther, *At Home in the World: A Rule of Life for the Rest of Us* (New York: Seabury Books, 2006), 7.

28. Ibid., 20.

29. Ibid.

30. Eric Dean, *Saint Benedict for the Laity* (Collegeville, MN: Liturgical Press, 1989), 11.

31. Ibid., 14.

32. Ibid., 19.

33. Ibid., 24.

34. Ibid., 96.

35. Ibid., 99.

36. Patrick Barry, *Saint Benedict's Rule* (York, UK: Ampleforth Abbey Press, 1997), 1.

37. Ibid., 5.

38. Ibid., 9.

39. Ibid., 10–11.

40. Patrick Barry, "A Short Introduction," in *The Benedictine Handbook*, ed. Anthony Marett-Crosby (Collegeville, MN: Liturgical Press, 2003), 5.

41. Dwight Longenecker, "Living the Rule as an Oblate," in *The Benedictine Handbook*, 297. See also 295–98 for content addressed.

42. Esther de Waal, "Living the Rule in the World," in *The Benedictine Handbook*, 301–2.

43. Ibid., 301–4.

44. Rachel Srubas, *Oblation: Meditations on St. Benedict's Rule* (Brewster, MA: Paraclete Press, 2006), xiii.

45. Ibid., xvi–xvii.

46. Ibid., xxiv.

47. Lonni Collins Pratt and Daniel Homan, *Benedict's Way: An Ancient Monk's Insights for a Balanced Life* (Chicago: Loyola Press, 2000), 12.

48. Ibid., 14.

49. Norvene Vest, *No Moment Too Small: Rhythms of Silence, Prayer and Holy Reading* (Boston: Cowley Publications, 1994), 3.

50. Ibid., 4.

51. Ibid., 6.

52. Ibid., 7.

53. Ibid., 8–9.

54. Norvene Vest, *Friend of the Soul: A Benedictine Spirituality of Work* (Boston: Cowley Publications, 1997), 17.

55. Pratt and Homan, *Benedict's Way* 11.

56. Vest, *No Moment Too Small*, 8.

57. Vest, *Friend of the Soul*, 2.

58. Esther de Waal, *A Life-Giving Way: A Commentary on the Rule of St. Benedict* (Collegeville, MN: Liturgical Press, 1995), vii.

59. Ibid., ix.

60. Ibid., xv.

61. Tomaine, quoting Steindl-Rast in *St. Benedict's Toolbox*, 5.

62. Tomaine, quoting de Waal in *St. Benedict's Toolbox*, 21.

63. Chittister, *Wisdom Distilled from the Daily: Living the Rule of St. Benedict Today* (New York: Harper & Row, 1990), 4.

64. Michael Casey, *An Unexciting Life: Reflections on Benedictine Spirituality* (Petersham, MA: Saint Bede's Publications, 2005), 449.

65. Ibid., 134.

66. Ibid., see pp. 129–54.

67. De Waal, "Living the Rule in the World," in *The Benedictine Handbook*, 304.

Chapter 3—pages 20–78

1. Anselm Grün, *Benedict of Nursia: His Message for Today*, trans. Linda M. Maloney (Collegeville, MN: Liturgical Press, 2006), 22.

2. Cyprian Smith, *The Path of Life: Benedictine Spirituality for Monks and Lay People* (1995; repr.,York: Ampleforth Abbey Press, 1996), 43.

3. Smith, *The Path of Life*, 57.

4. Columba Stewart, *Prayer and Community: The Benedictine Tradition* (Maryknoll, NY: Orbis Books, 1998), 32.

5. Ibid., 37.

6. De Waal, *A Life-Giving Way*, 56.

7. Chittister, quoted in Pratt and Homan, *Benedict's Way*, 39.

8. Pratt and Homan, *Benedict's Way*, 41.

9. Ibid., 42.

10. Julian of Norwich, quoted by Eric Dean in *Saint Benedict for the Laity*, 51.

11. Stewart, *Prayer and Community*, 69.

12. Pratt and Homan, *Benedict's Way*, 69.

13. De Waal, *Seeking God*, 121.

14. Chittister, *Wisdom Distilled from the Daily*, 130–31.

15. Vest, *No Moment Too Small*, 21.

16. Ibid., 22.

17. Smith, *The Path of Life*, 59.

18. *The American Heritage Dictionary*, 2nd college edition (Boston: Houghton Mifflin Company, 1985), s.v. "authentic."

19. Ronald Rolheiser, *The Restless Heart: Finding Our Spiritual Home* (New York: Doubleday, 2004), 133.

20. Grün, *Benedict of Nursia*, 47.

21. Chittister, *Wisdom Distilled from the Daily*, see 188–90.

22. Johann von Goethe, *The Maxims and Reflections of Goethe*, trans. T. Bailey Saunders (New York: The Macmillan Company, 1906), available at Project Gutenberg, http://www.gutenberg.org/files/33670/33670-h/33670-h.htm.

23. Chittister, *The Rule of Benedict*, 150.

24. Andrew Greeley, "The Apologetics of Beauty," http://www.agreeley.com/articles/beauty.html.

25. Susan Marie Lindstrom, "Inside Every Monastic Is an Artist Waiting to Create," *Benedictines* 63, no. 1 (Spring/Summer 2010): 10.

26. Barbara Mayer, quoting Joan Chittister in *Benedictines* 63, no. 1 (Spring/Summer 2010): 4.

27. Greeley, "The Apologetics of Beauty."

28. John O'Donohue, *Beauty: The Invisible Embrace* (New York: Harper Perennial, 2005), 2.

29. The chapter in this book on the "History of Oblation" should clarify why there are such young boys in the monastery.

30. Michael Casey, "The Art of *Lectio Divina*," *The Benedictine Handbook*, ed. Anthony Marett-Crosby (Collegeville, MN: Liturgical Press, 2003), 107.

31. Chittister, *Wisdom Distilled from the Daily*, 104.

32. Katharine Le Mee, *The Benedictine Gift to Music* (New York: Paulist Press, 2003), 127.

33. Demetrius Dumm, *Cherish Christ Above All: The Bible in the Rule of Benedict* (New York: Paulist Press, 1996), 60–61; emphasis original.

Chapter 4—pages 79–95

1. Pope Gregory the Great, *The Dialogues,* book 2: *Life and Miracles of St. Benedict*, trans. Odo J. Zimmermann and Benedict R. Avery (Collegeville, MN: Liturgical Press, 1949), 16.

2. Penelope D. Johnson, *Equal in Monastic Profession: Religious Women in Medieval France* (Chicago: University of Chicago Press, 1991), 14–15. Judith Sutera, quoting Abbé Deroux in "The Origins of Benedictine Oblation in the Research of Abbé Deroux," *The American Benedictine Review* 52, no. 1 (March 2001): 25.

3. Derek G. Smith, "Oblates in Western Monasticism" in *Monastic Studies*, no. 13 (Autumn 1982): 51.

4. Ibid., 52.

5. Johnson, *Equal in Monastic Profession*, 15, 23.

6. Ibid., 16.

7. Ibid., 22.

8. Ibid., 19.

9. Ibid., 26.

10. Stephanus Hilpisch, in *New Catholic Encyclopedia* (New York: McGraw-Hill Book Company, 1967), s.v. "oblates."

11. *Manual for Oblates of St. Benedict* (Collegeville, MN: Saint John's Abbey Press), 3–4.

12. Hilpisch, in *New Catholic Encyclopedia*, s.v. "conversi."

13. Johnson, *Equal in Monastic Profession*, 47.

14. Ibid., 42, 33.

15. Smith, "Oblates in Western Monasticism," 53.

16. Ibid., 54.

17. Sutera, "The Origins of Benedictine Oblation," 28.

18. Ibid., 29.

19. *Manual for Oblates of St. Benedict*, 4.

20. Hugh Feiss, "Henry II: Monk-King," *Benedict in the World* (Collegeville, MN: Liturgical Press, 2002), 105.

21. Ibid., 115.

22. Thomas Bokenkotter, *A Concise History of the Catholic Church*, rev. ed. (New York: Random House / Doubleday, 2004), 201.

23. Ibid., 201.

24. Smith, "Oblates in Western Monasticism," 62.

25. Ibid., 66.

26. Alan Schreck, *The Compact History of the Catholic Church* (Ann Arbor, MI: Servant Books, 1987), 61.

27. Ibid., 61.

28. Barrie Ruth Straus, *The Catholic Church* (New York: Hippocrene Books, 1987), 87.

29. Straus, *The Catholic Church*, 89–90.

30. Schreck, *Compact History*, 62.

31. There were calls for reform of the Catholic Church in the 14th and 15th centuries, but the failures to achieve them are not addressed in the content of this book. Consequently, to convey the more successful efforts at Catholic Reformation, we have adapted the dates 1500–1650 given by Schreck in *The Compact History of the Catholic Church*, p. 69. The same source is used for the dates given for the "Modern World," p. 79. To do justice to these topics the reader is referred to scholarly and detailed publications of choice.

32. Ibid., 71–73.

33. A. G. Biggs in *New Catholic Encyclopedia*, vol. 2 (New York: McGraw-Hill Book Company, 1967), s.v. "Benedictines."

34. Schreck, *Compact History*, 87.

35. Smith, "Oblates in Western Monasticism," 71.

36. See for example such sources as Roger Aubert, Johannes Beckmann, Patrick J. Corish, and Rudolf Lill, *The Church between Revolution and Restoration*, trans. Peter Becker, vol. 7 of *History of the Church*, ed. Hubert Jedin and John Dolan (New York: Crossroad, 1981), 3–76; A. Latreille, *French Revolution*, vol. 6 of *New Catholic Encyclopedia* (New York: McGraw-Hill Book Company, 1967), 186–93; Bokenkotter, A *Concise History of the Catholic Church*, 280–93.

37. Schreck, *Compact History*, 94.

38. Oblate Formation Booklet, Saint Vincent Archabbey, 53, http://www.svaoblates.org/files/OblateFormation.pdf.

39. Abbot Alcuin Deutsch, *Manual for Oblates of St. Benedict*, 3rd ed. (Collegeville, MN: Saint John's Abbey Press, 1948), 23–24.

40. Colman J. Barry, *Worship and Work* (Collegeville, MN: Liturgical Press, 1980), 150.

41. Sr. Alfreda had first attended Notre Dame University in 1931, and then again in 1937.

42. The Sodality was a key spiritual organization in the college at this time and even into the 1960s.

43. "For at least thirty years the College of St. Benedict has promoted and encouraged young women students of the College to become Oblates of St. Benedict. Quite frequently our lay employees are also interested in becoming Oblates" (Mother Henrita Osendorf to the Right Reverend Benno Gut, 15 January 1962, Saint Benedict's Monastery archives, St. Joseph, MN). All following letters in this chapter were accessed from this archive.

44. The true founding of this association was 1949 as noted in A-5 of NAABOD, *Handbook for Directors of Benedictine Oblates* (Saint Meinrad, IN: Abbey Press, 2000).

45. NAABOD, *Handbook for Directors*, A-10.

Chapter 5—pages 96–104

1. Walter M. Abbot, ed., *Gaudium et Spes, The Documents of Vatican II* (New York: America Press, 1966), 244. All references to Vatican II documents are cited from this edition.

2. Martin H. Work, "Laity," *The Documents of Vatican II*, 486.

3. Ibid., citing Pope Paul VI, 488.

4. Ronald Rolheiser, *Secularity and the Gospel: Being Missionaries to our Children* (Chestnut Ridge, NY: Crossroad, 2006).

Chapter 6—pages 105–10

1. Father Bede Classick, "The Benedictine Oblate Life," in NAABOD, *A Handbook for Directors*, C-1.

2. Director of Oblates, et al., *Oblate Formation Booklet for Oblates of Saint Benedict Affiliated with Saint Vincent Archabbey* (Latrobe, PA: Saint Vincent Archabbey, 1995), http://www.osb.org/sva/obl/pdf/OblateFormation.pdf, 28.

3. "The Benedictine Oblate Life," in NAABOD, *Handbook for Directors*, C-2.

4. The quotes and essences of the guideline contents are taken from NAABOD, *Handbook for Directors*, C-11–C-15.

Appendix A—pages 130–32

1. North American Association of Benedictine Oblate Directors, *A Handbook for Directors of Benedictine Oblates* (St. Meinrad, IN: Abbey Press, 2000), C-1 and C-2.

2. Appendix D in *A Handbook for Directors of Benedictine Oblates*.

Appendix C (alternate 1)—page 141

1. Macrina Wiederkehr, OSB, *The Song of the Seed* (New York: HarperCollins, 1995), 12–19.

Appendix D—page 144

1. Alexius Hoffmann, *A Benedictine Martyrology* (Collegeville, MN: Saint John's Abbey Press, 1922).

Appendix E—pages 169–74

1. Summarized from "The Medal of Saint Benedict" (Collegeville, MN: Liturgical Press, 2008).

2. "The Medal of Saint Benedict."

3. Ibid. (summarized).

4. "The Medal of Saint Benedict."

5. Judith Sutera, ed., *Word of God: Benedictine Prayer* (Collegeville, MN: Liturgical Press, 1997), 104.

6. Quoted in *The Work of God*, ed. Judith Sutera (Collegeville, MN; Liturgical Press, 1997), 105–6.